Amazing Animals

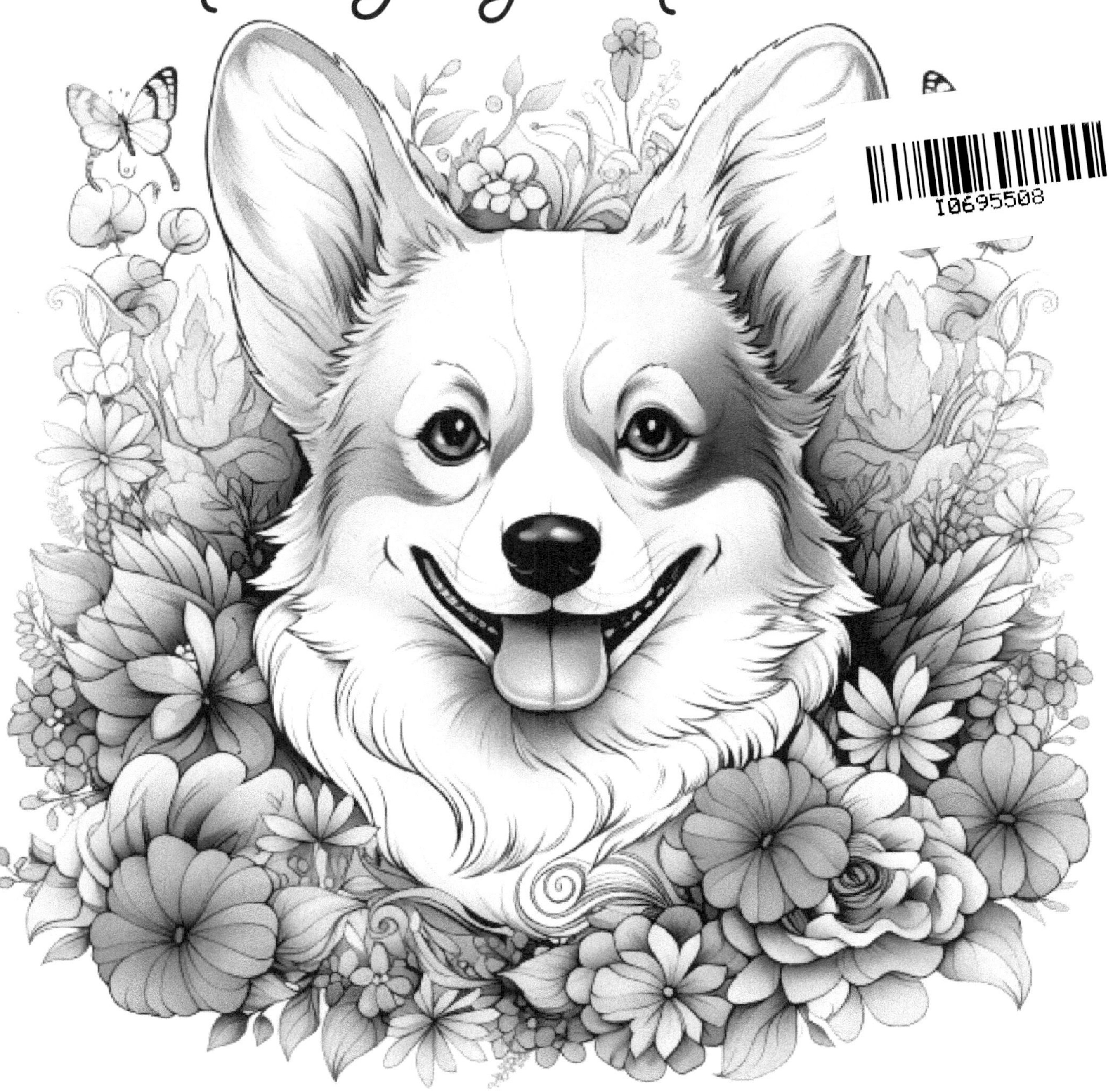

AN ANIMAL LOVER'S COLORING BOOK

By Neil Dubey

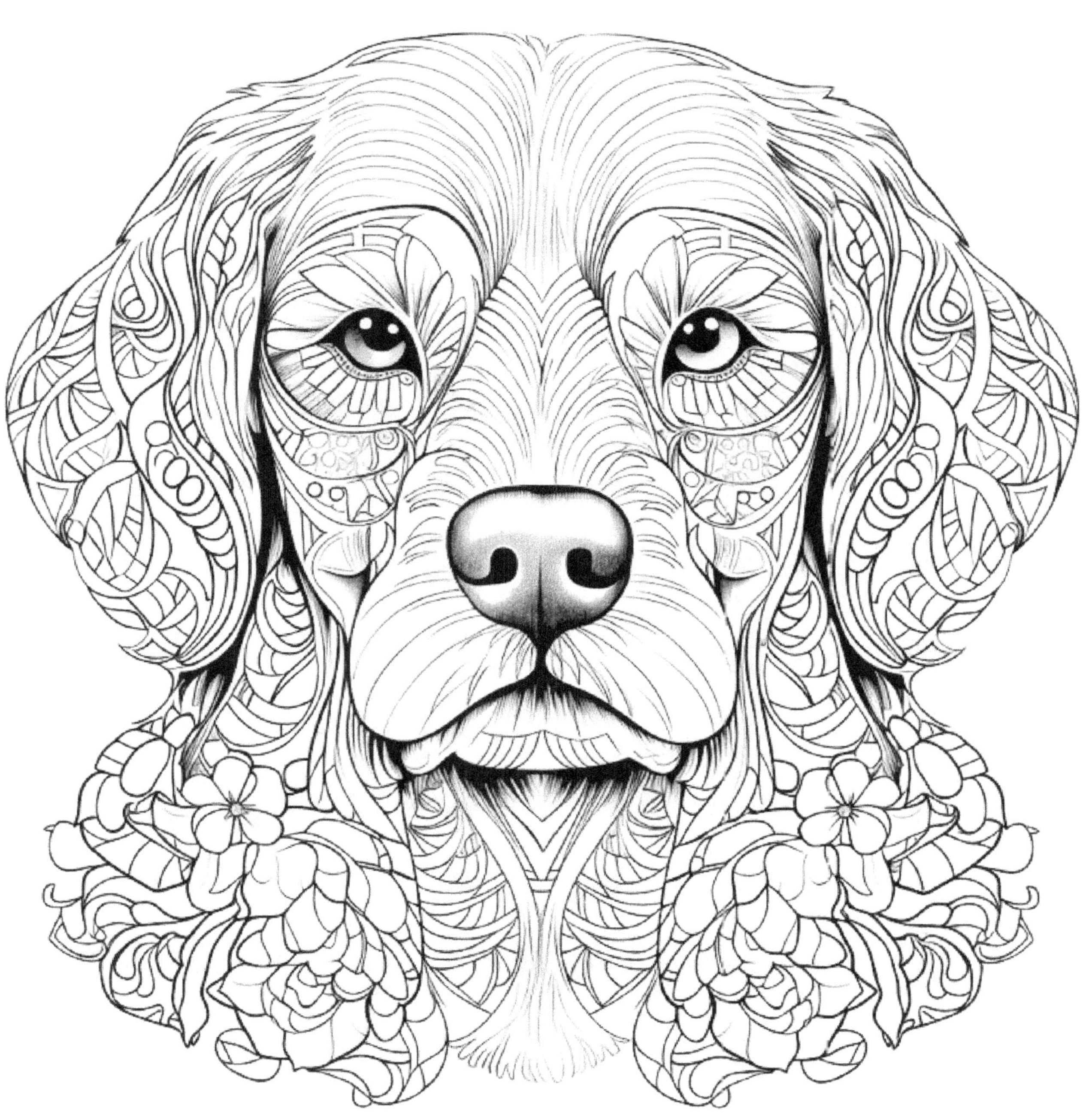

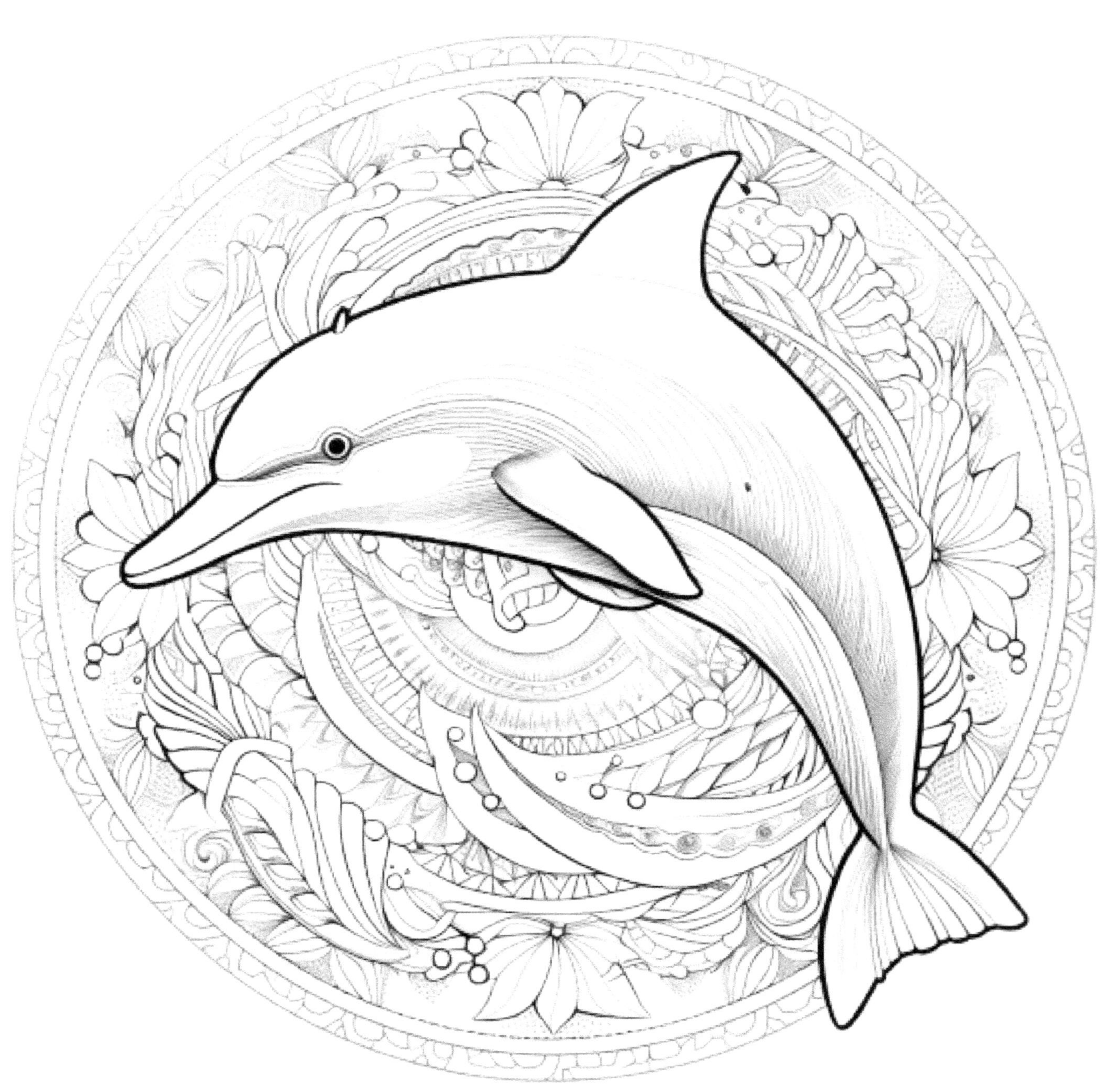

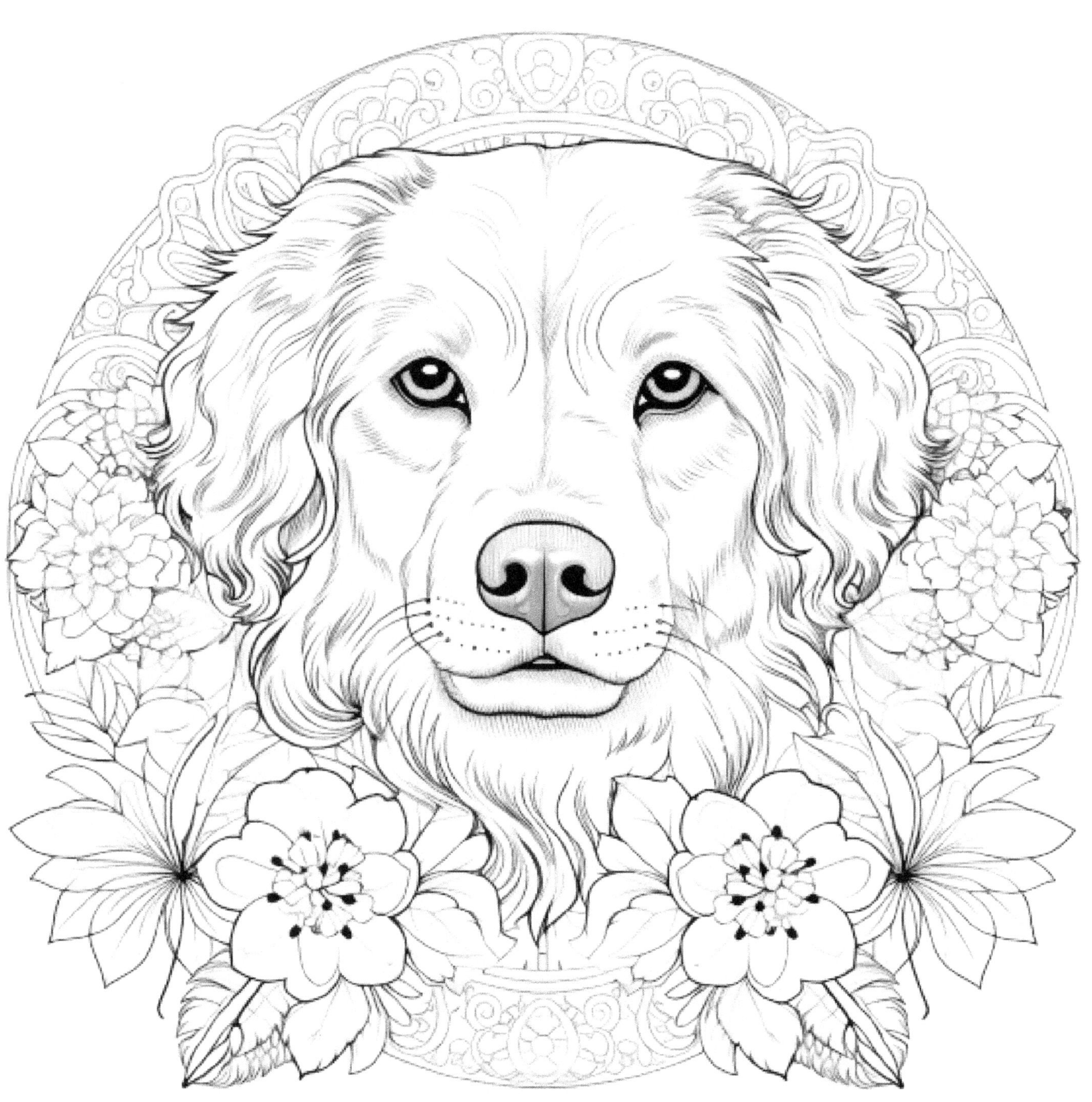

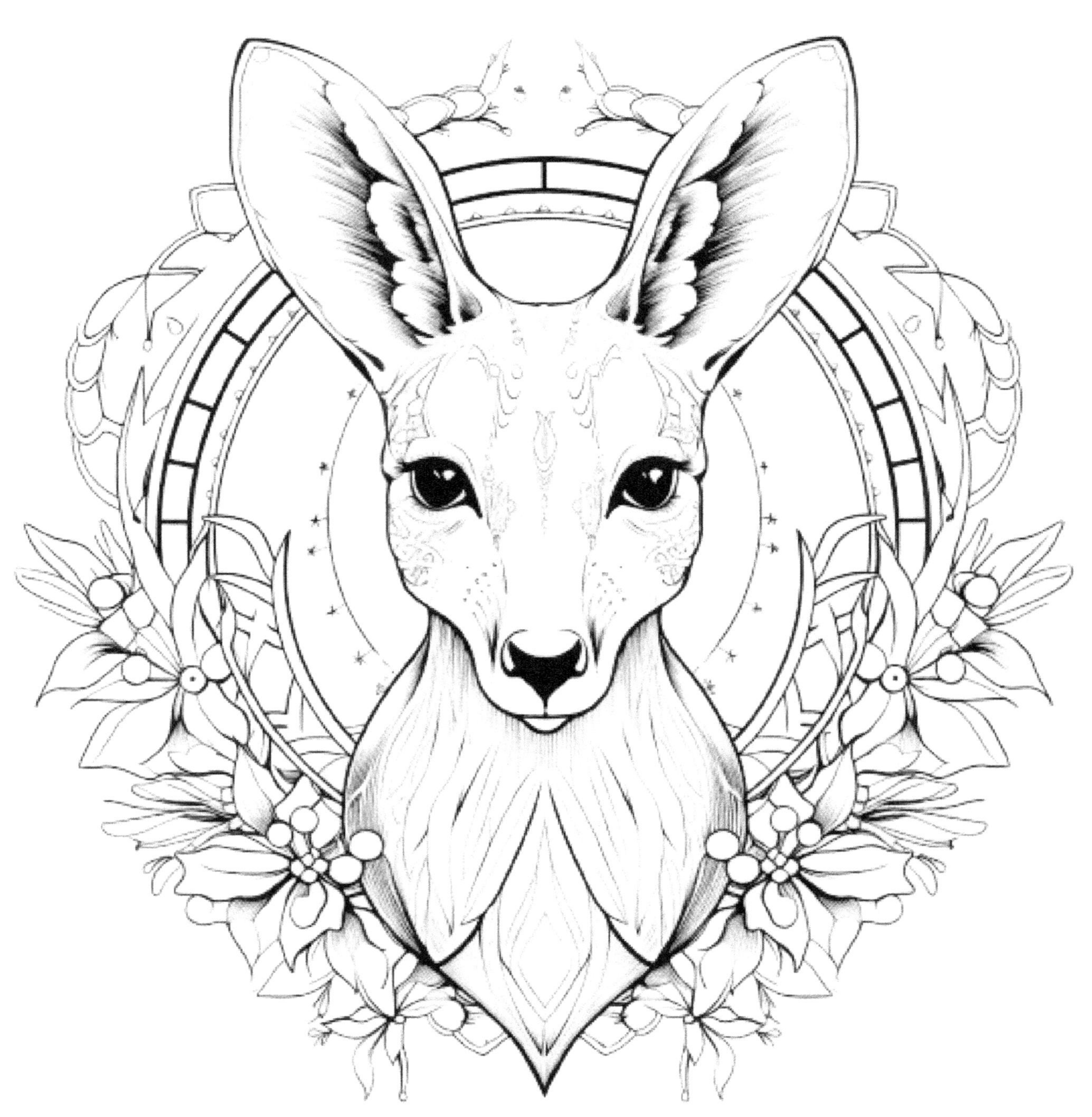

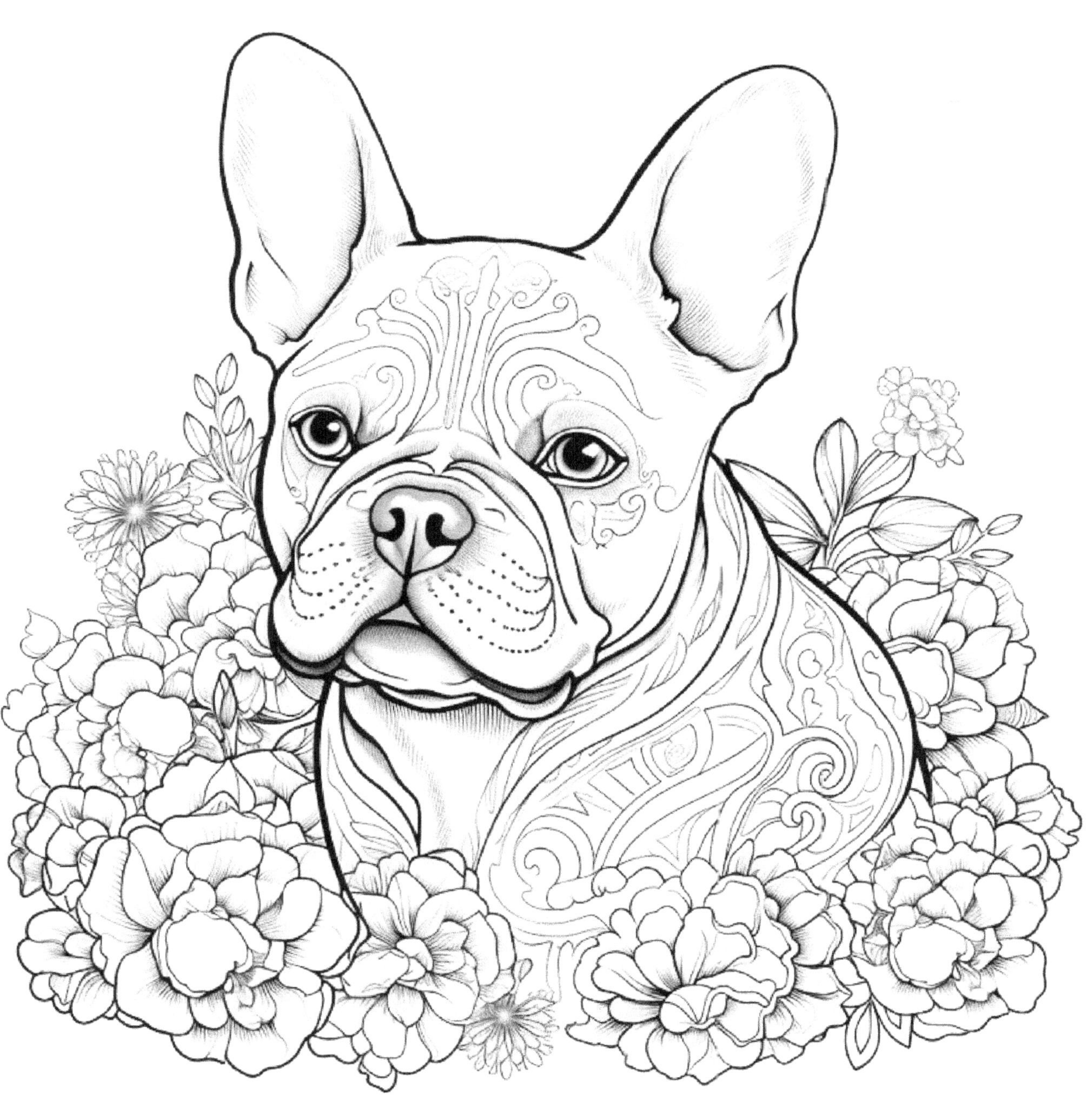

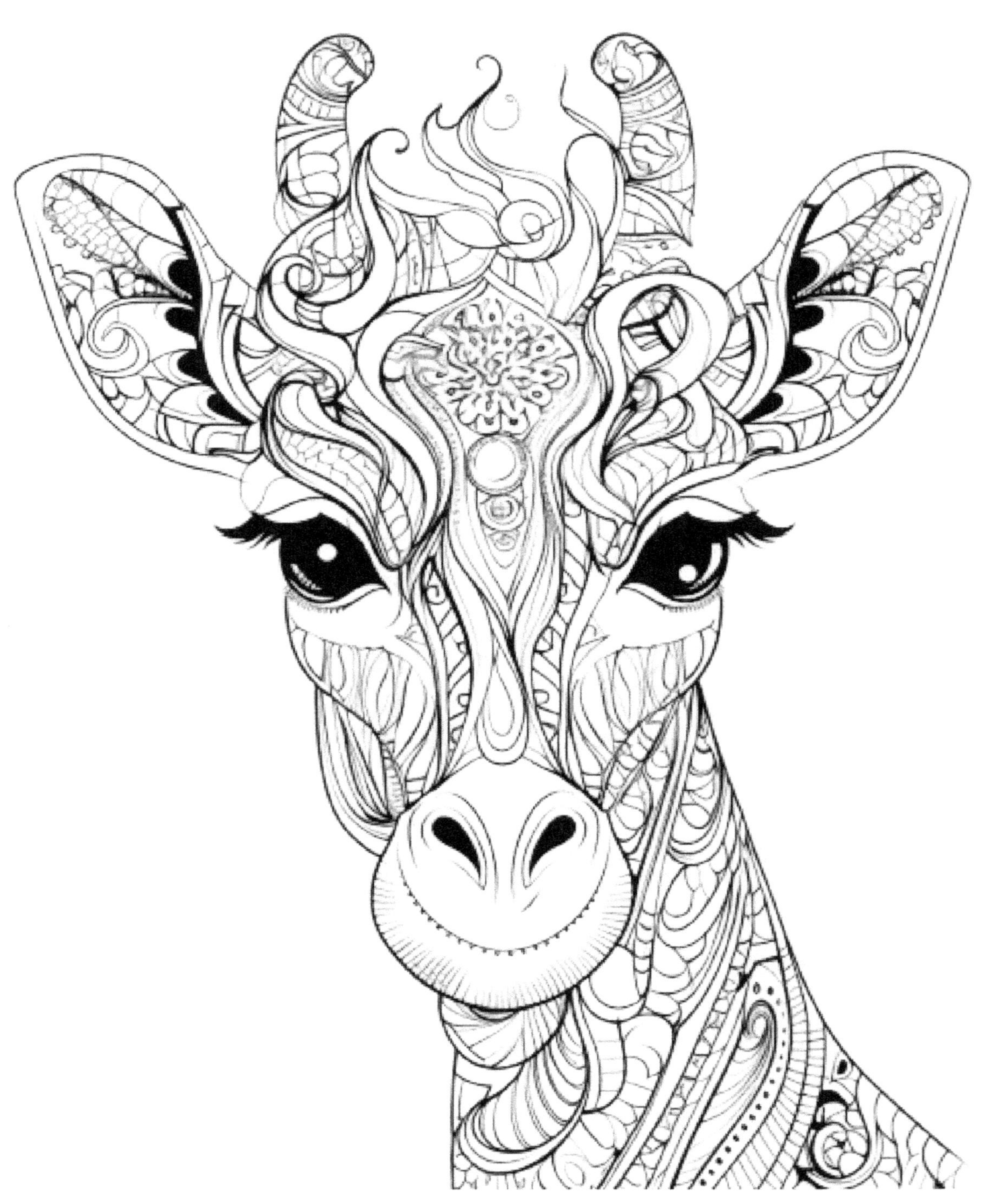

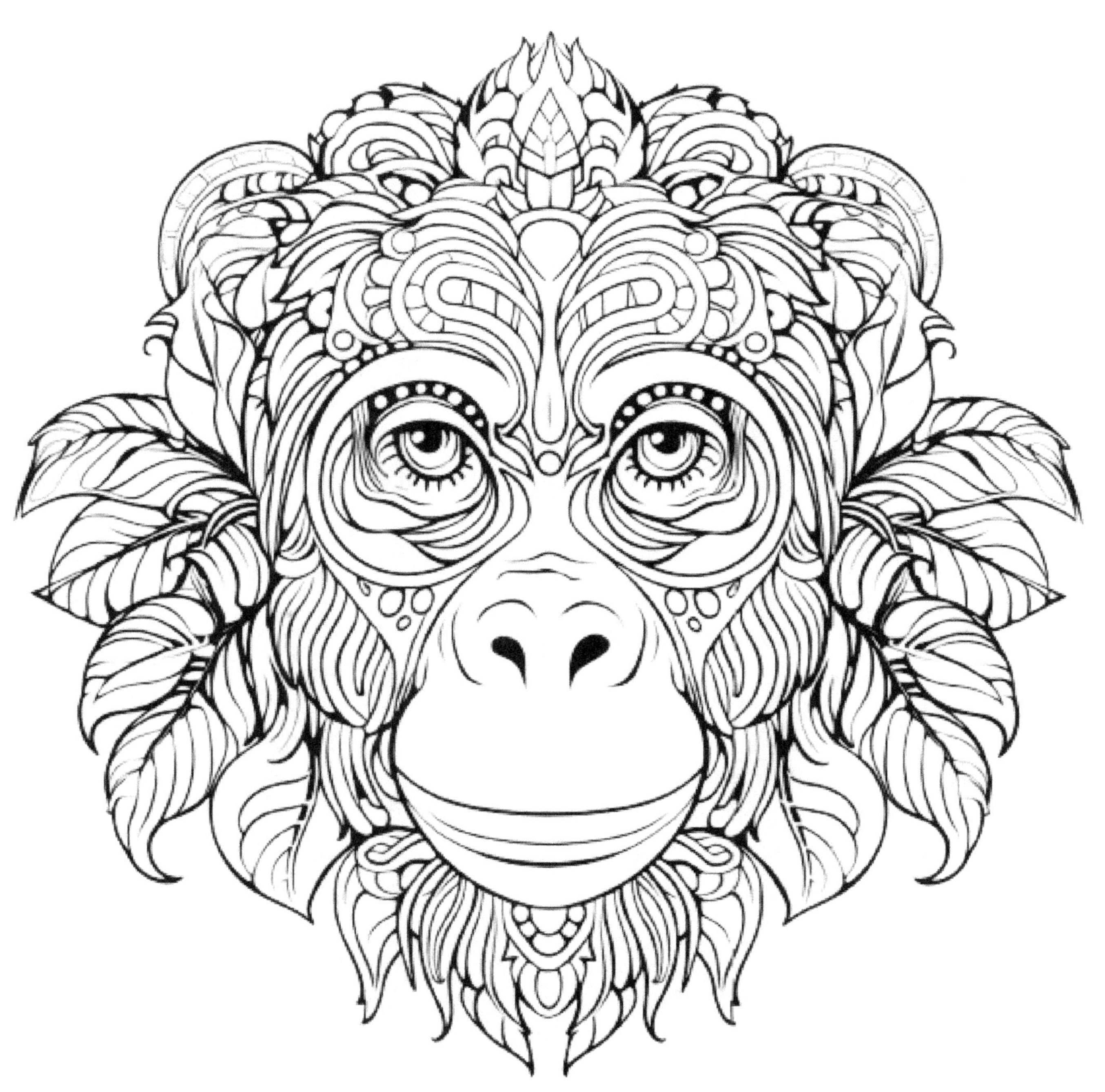

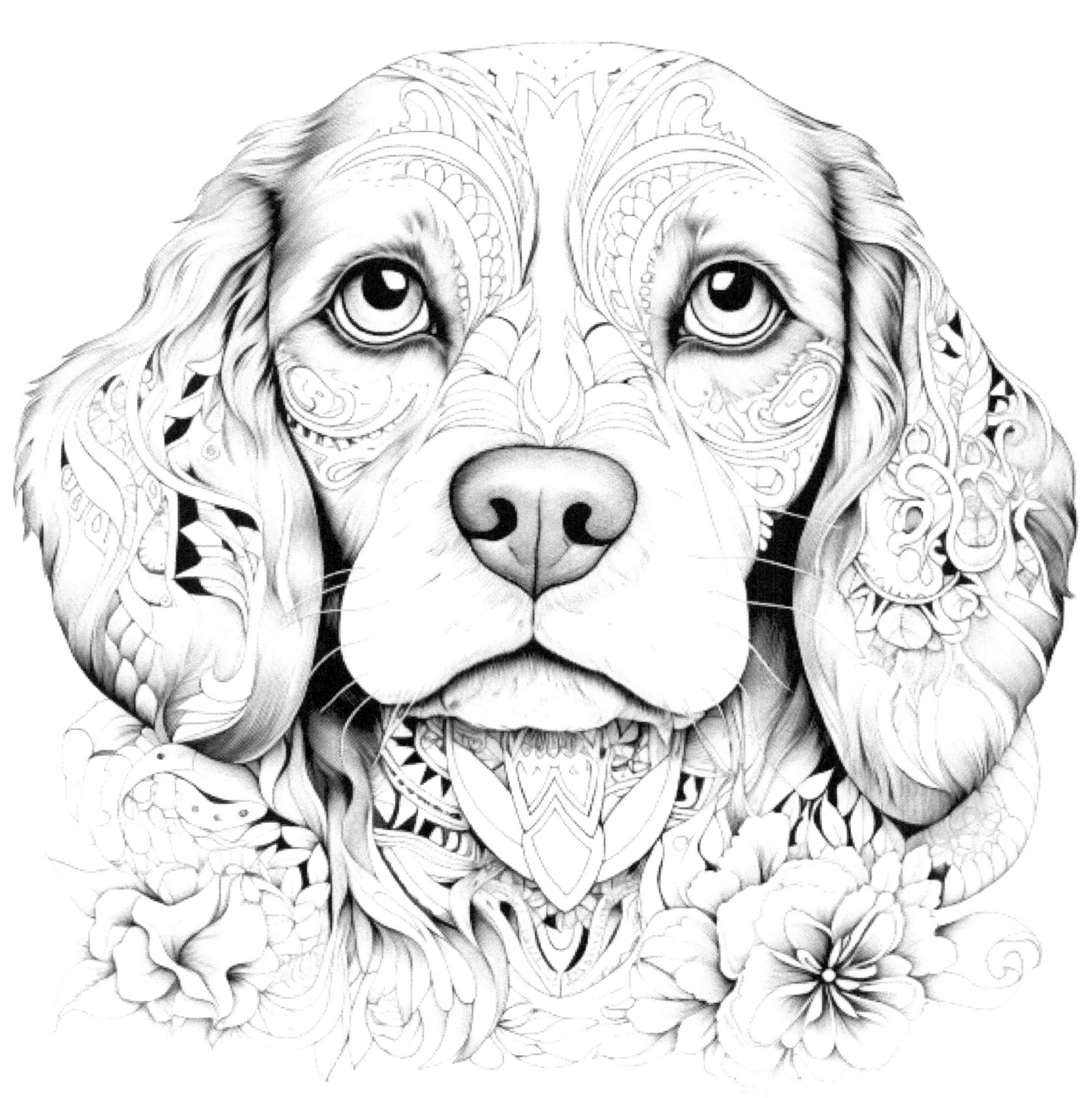

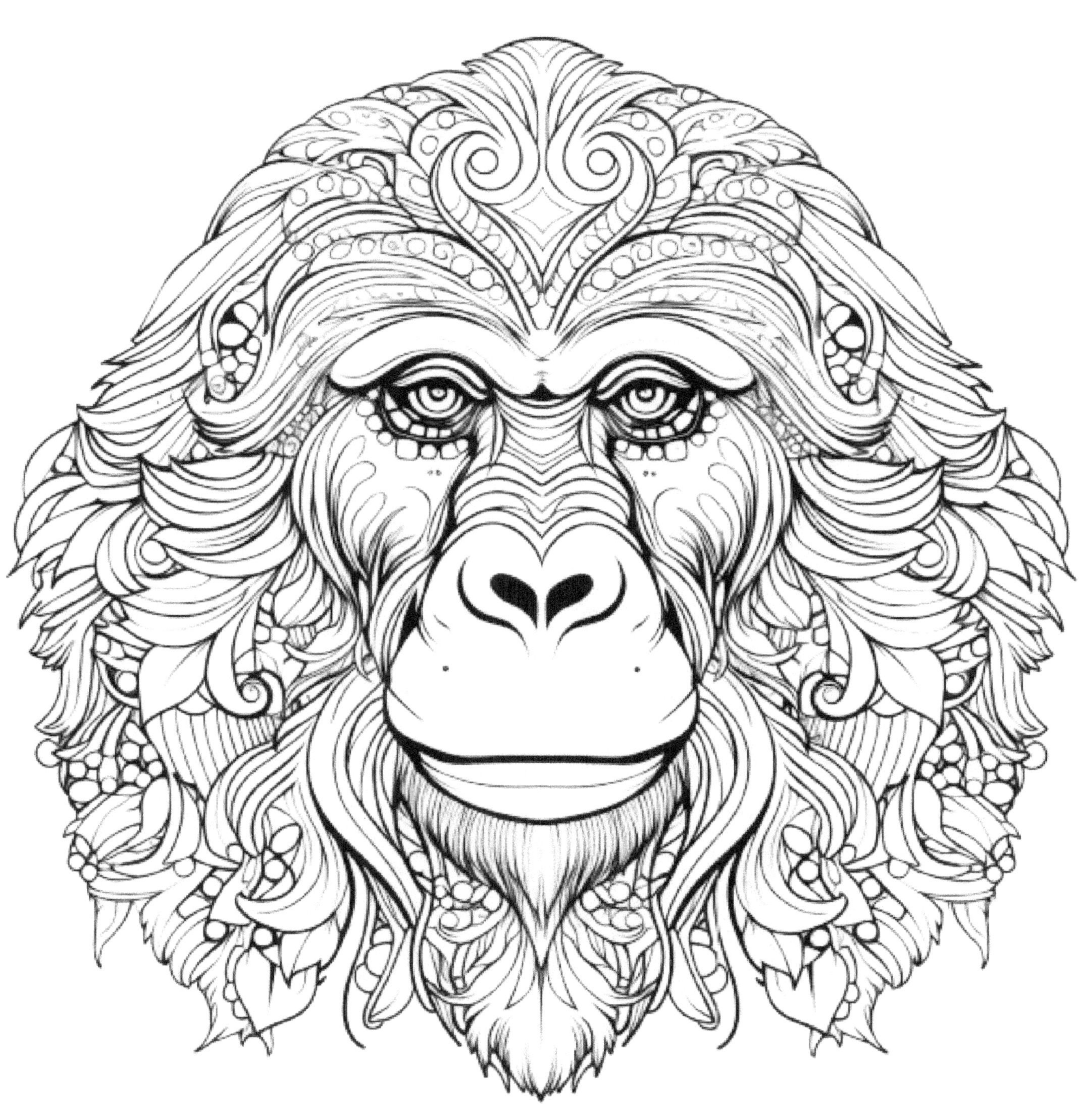

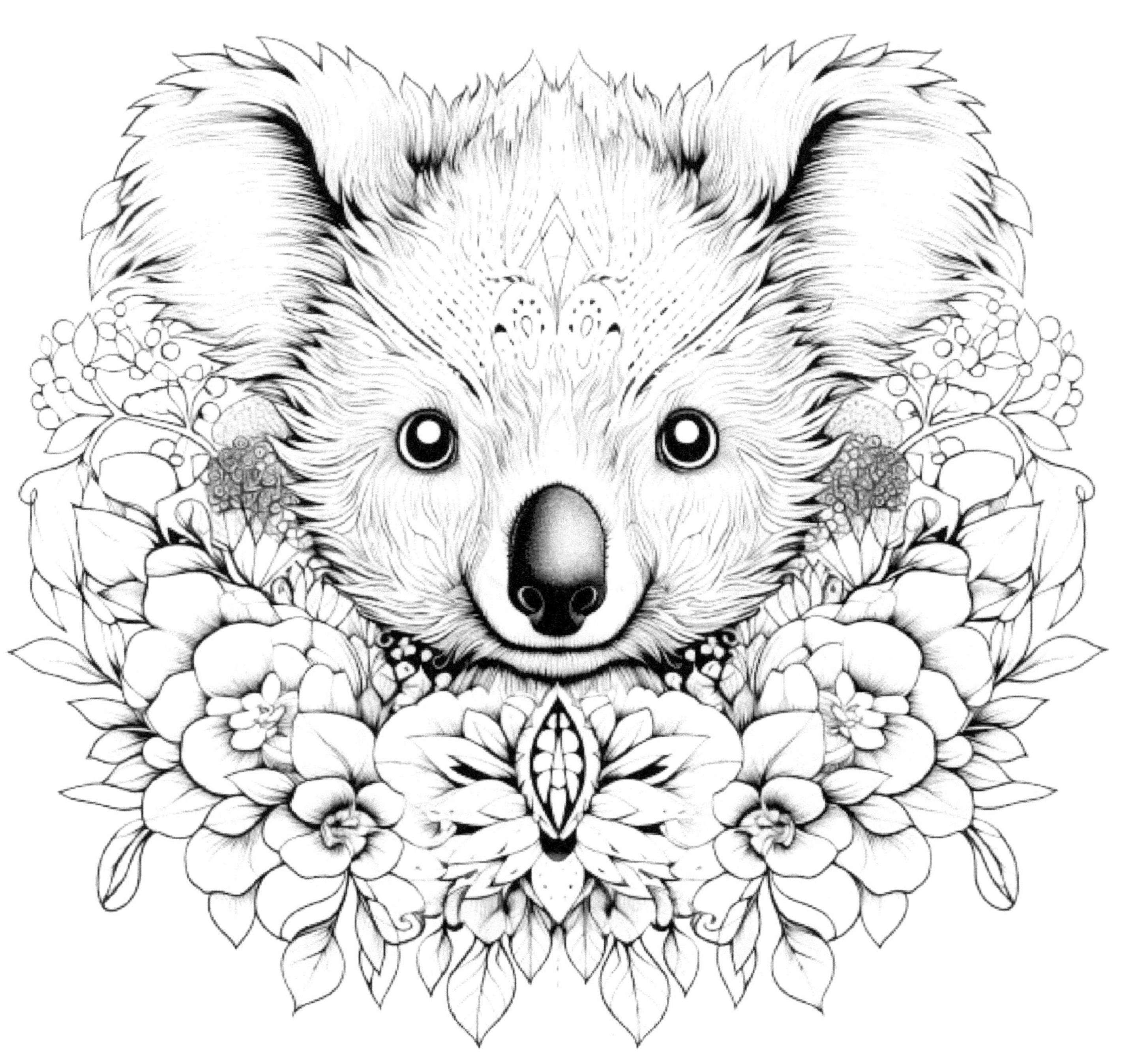

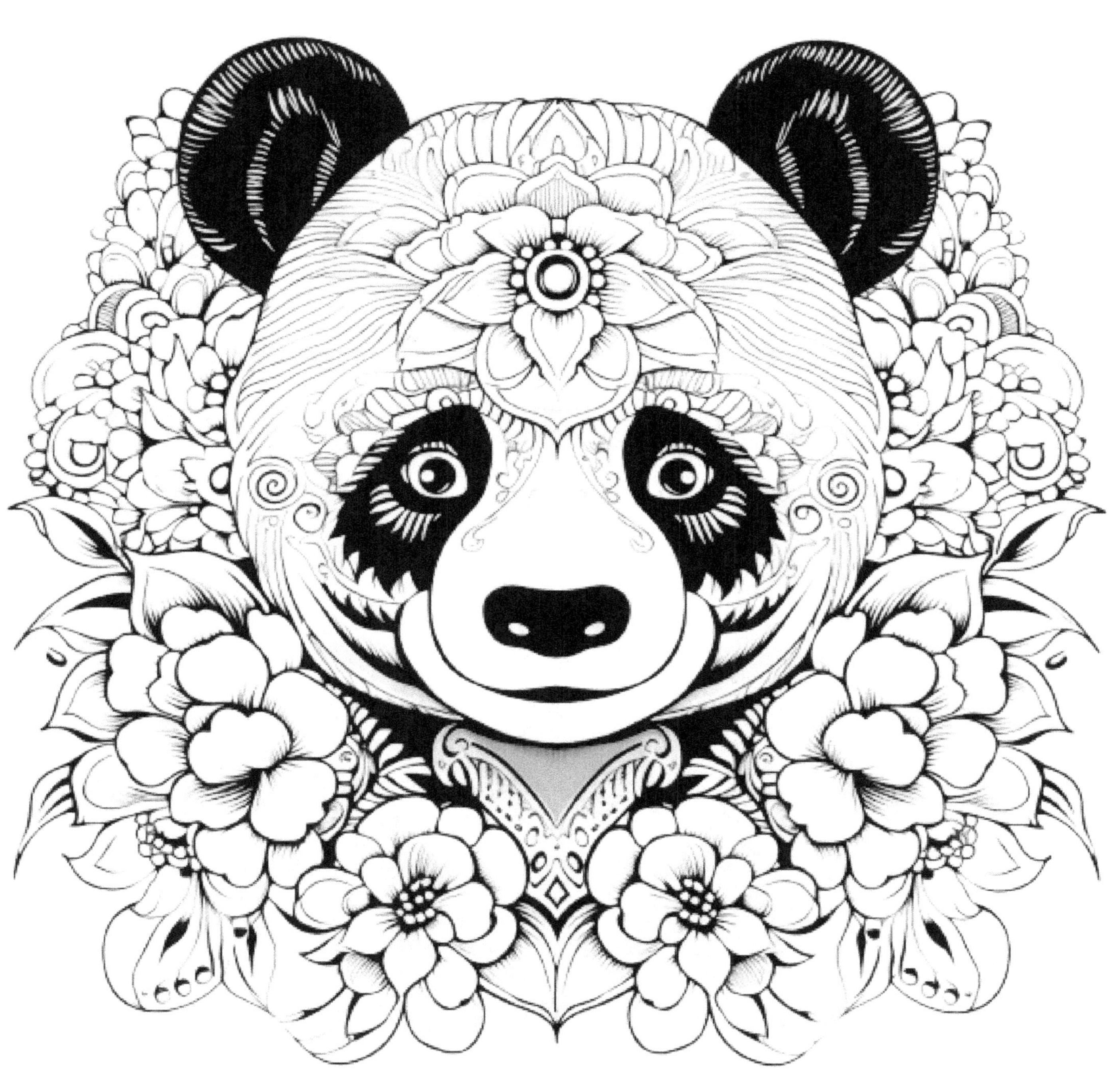

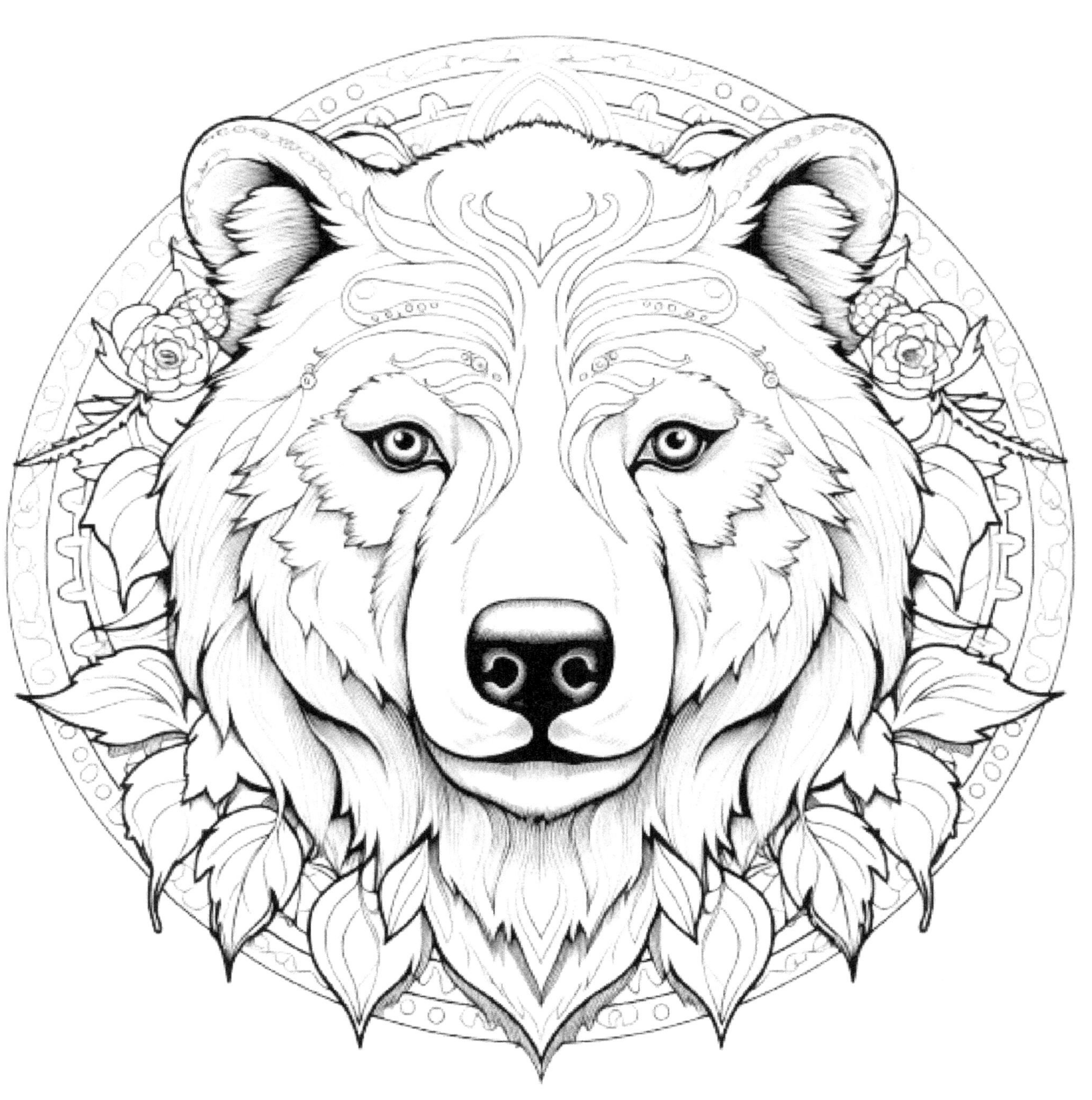

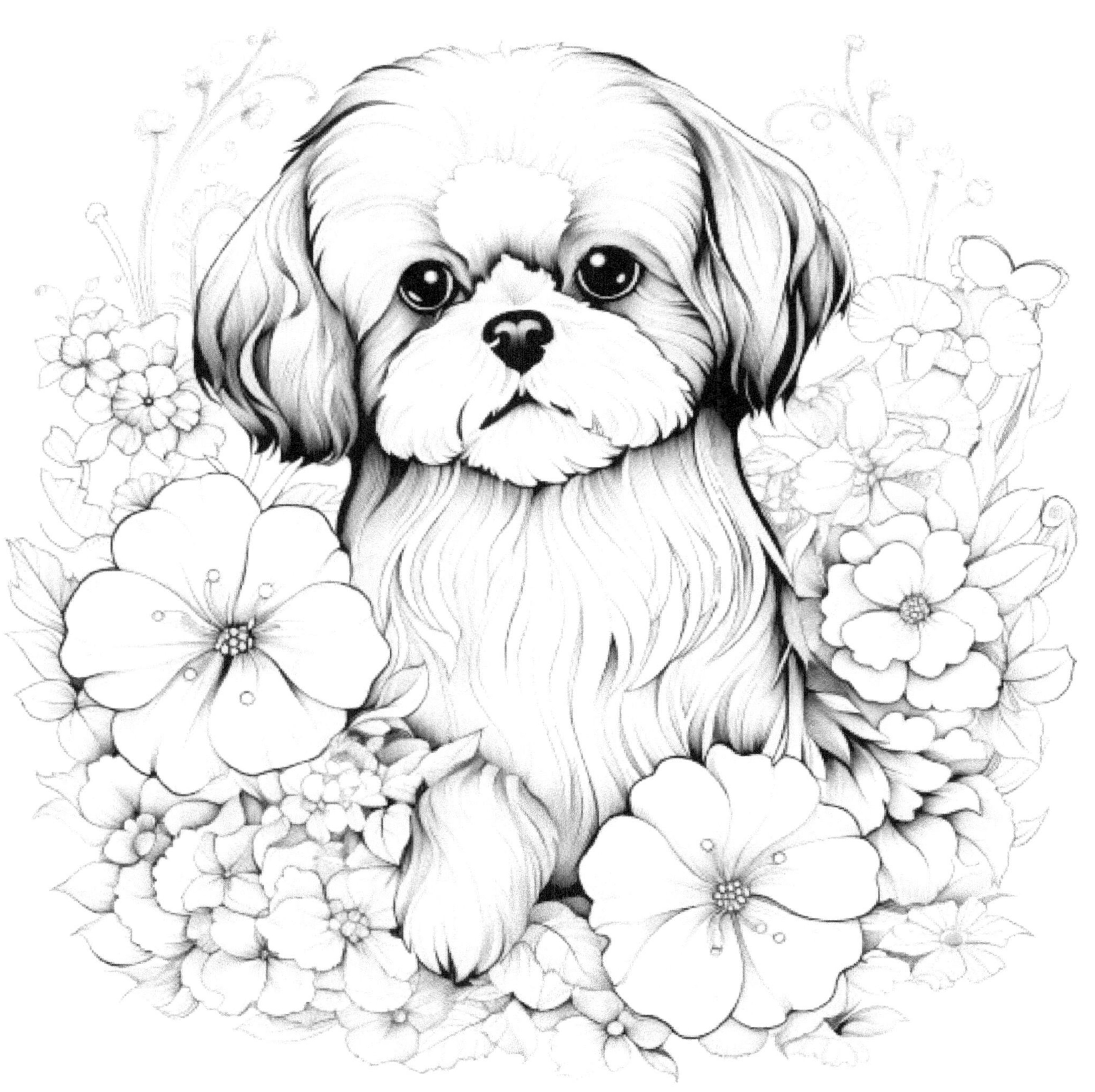

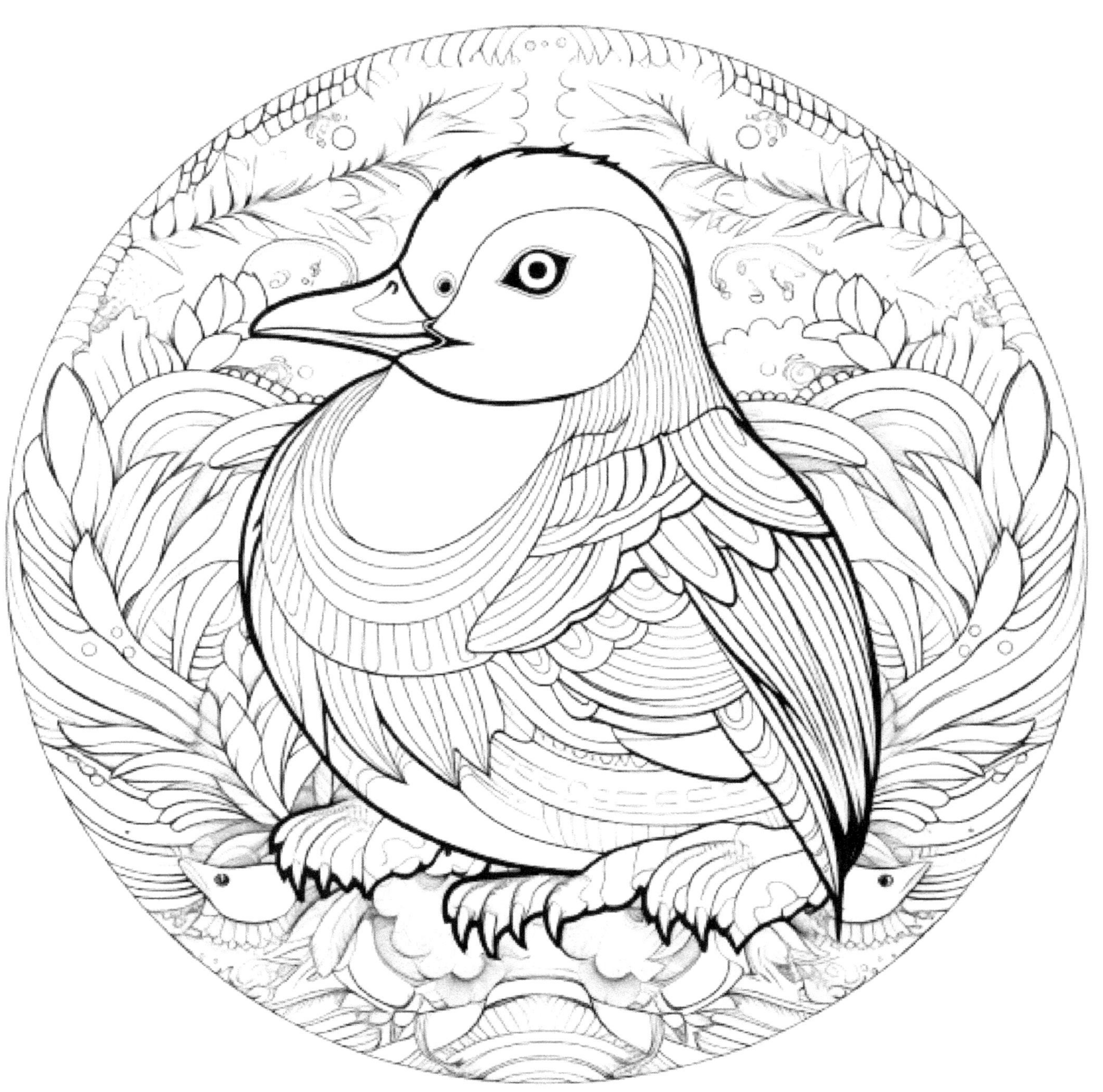

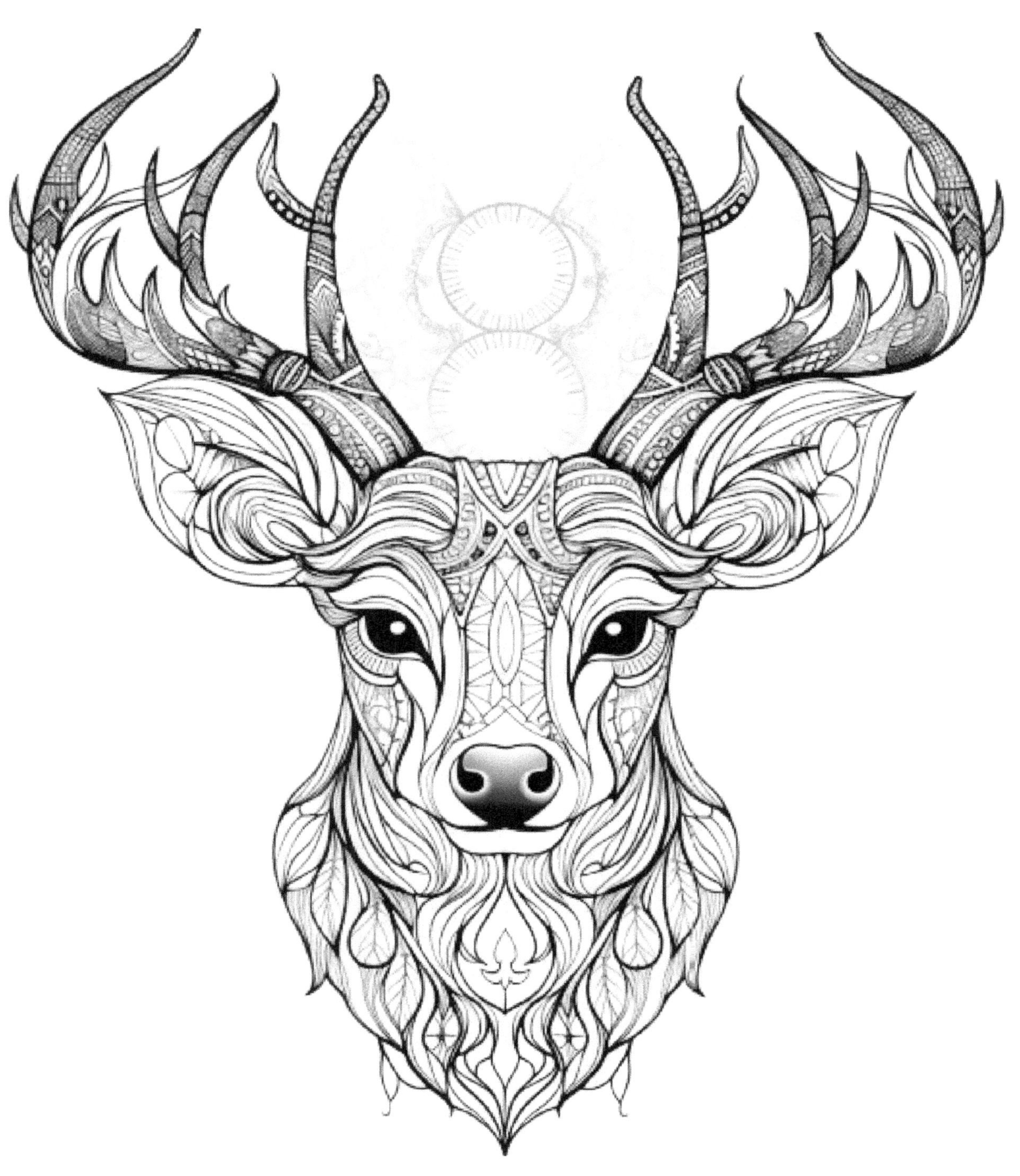

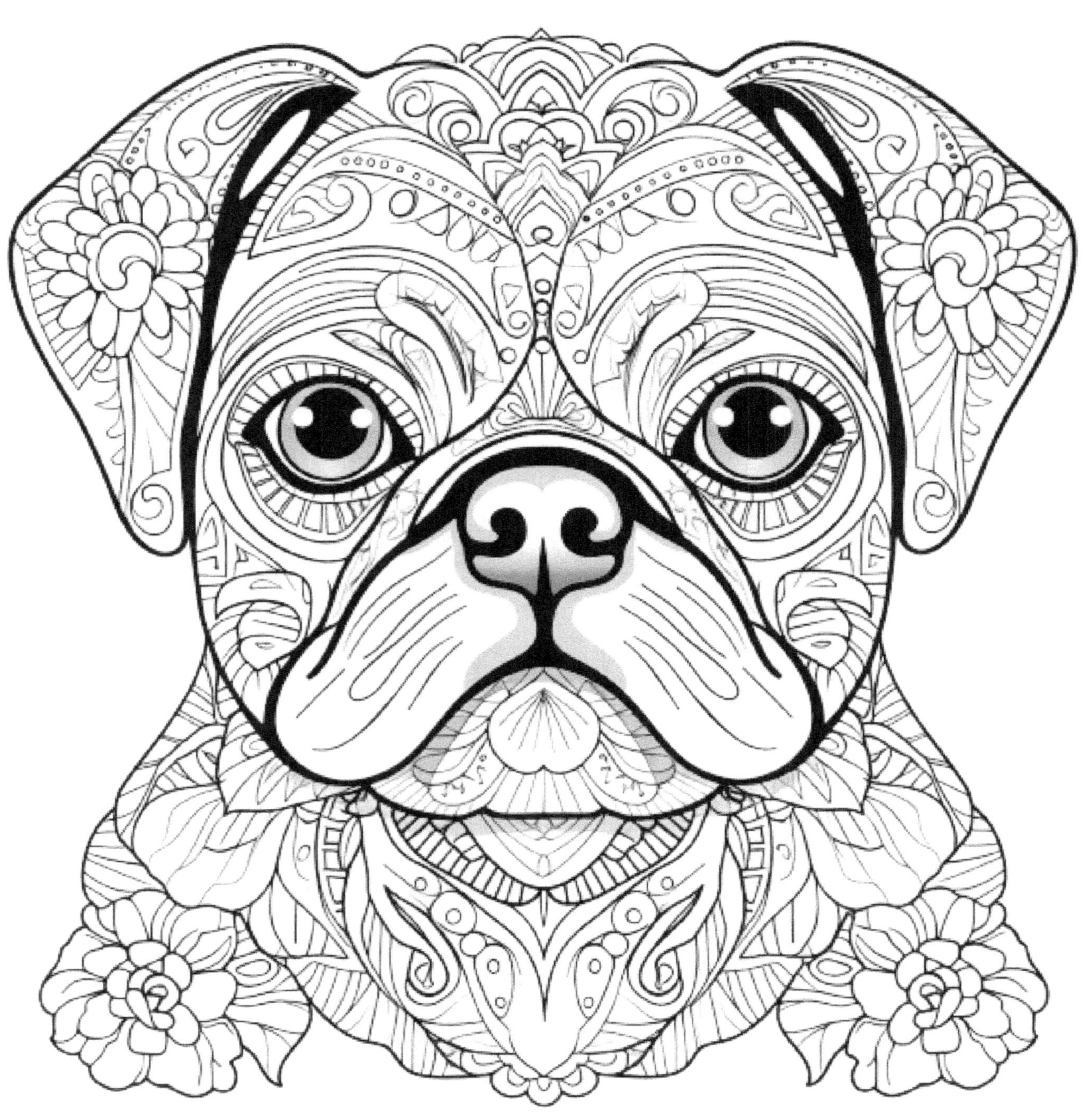

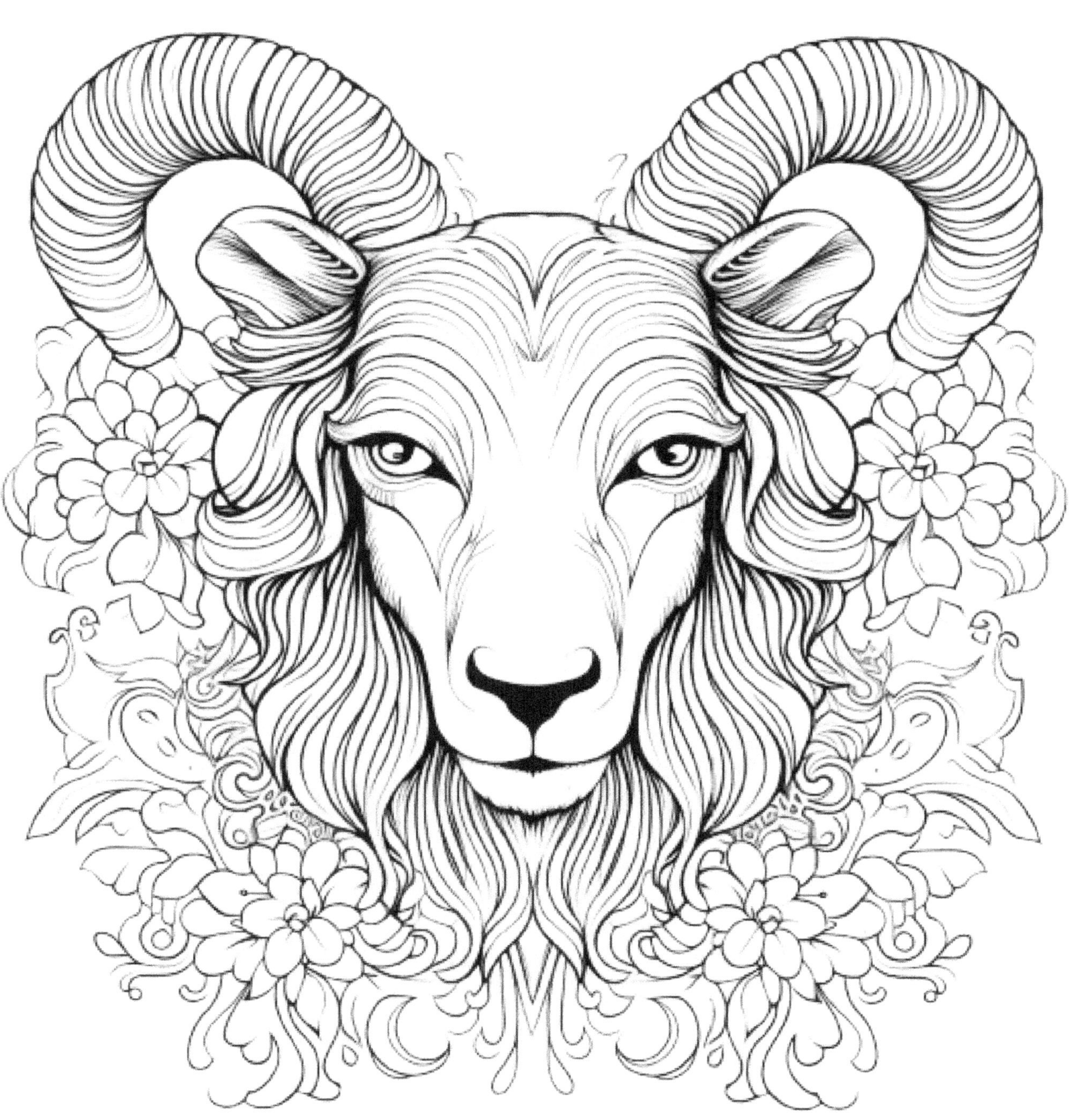

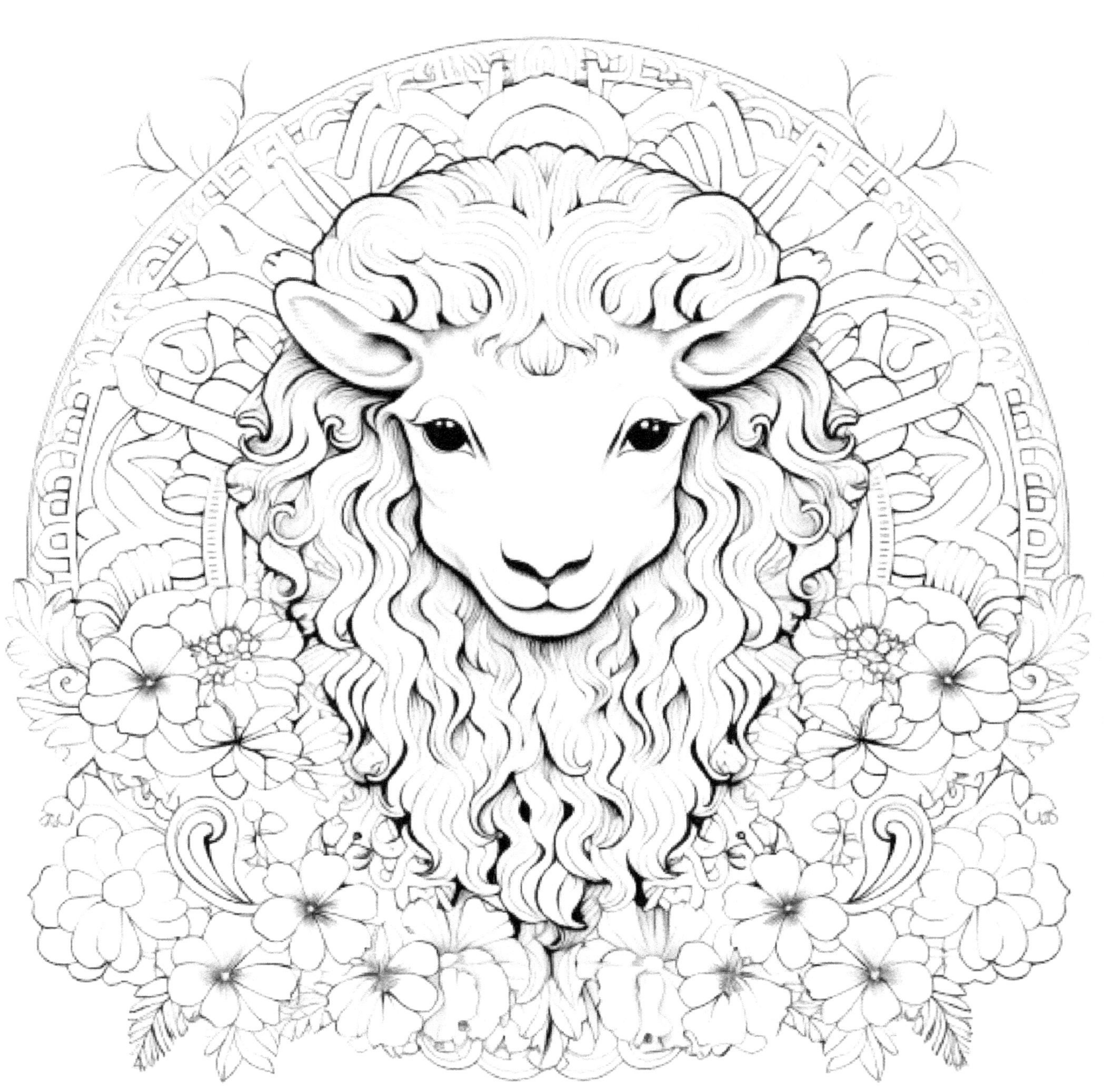

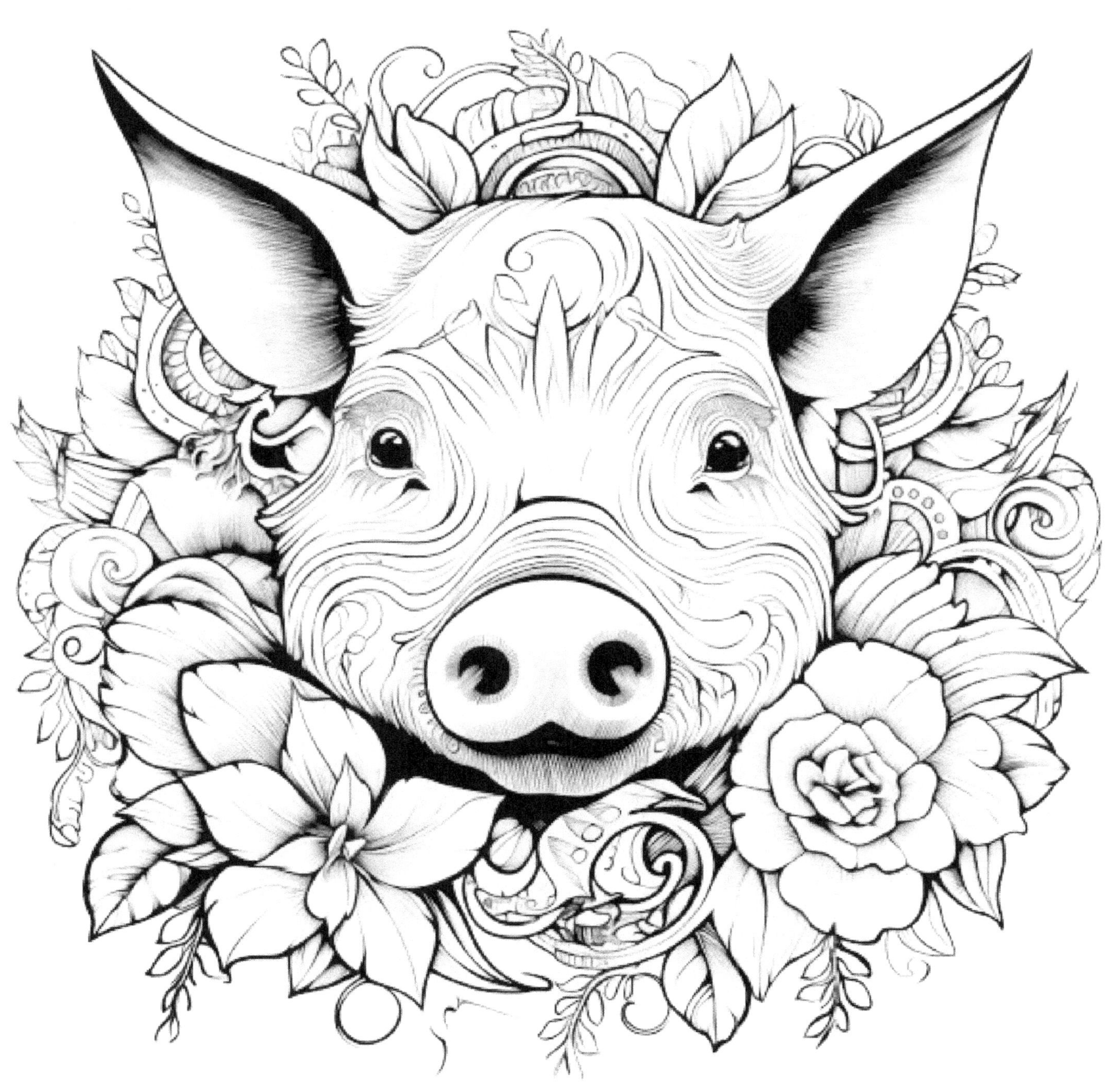

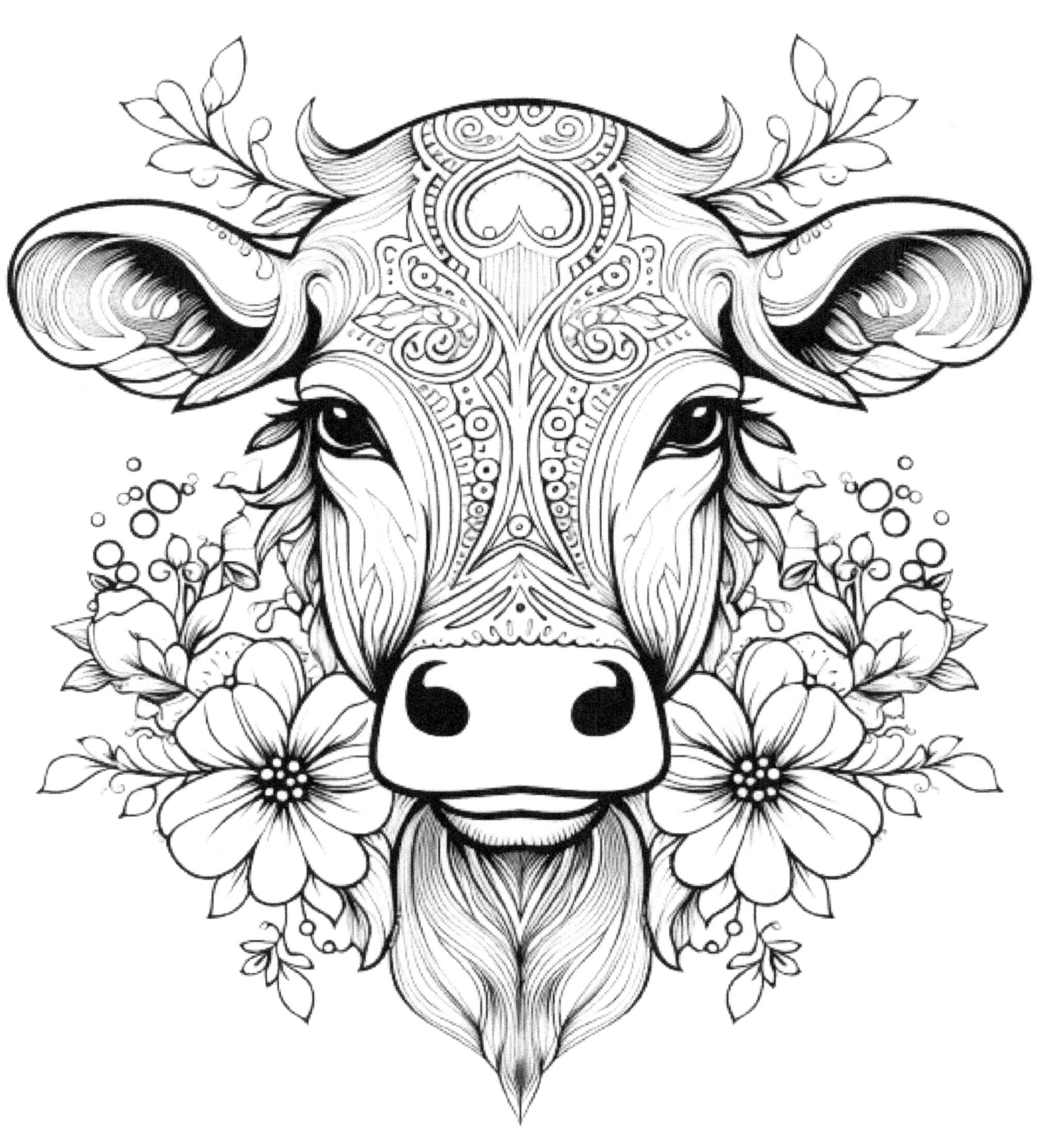

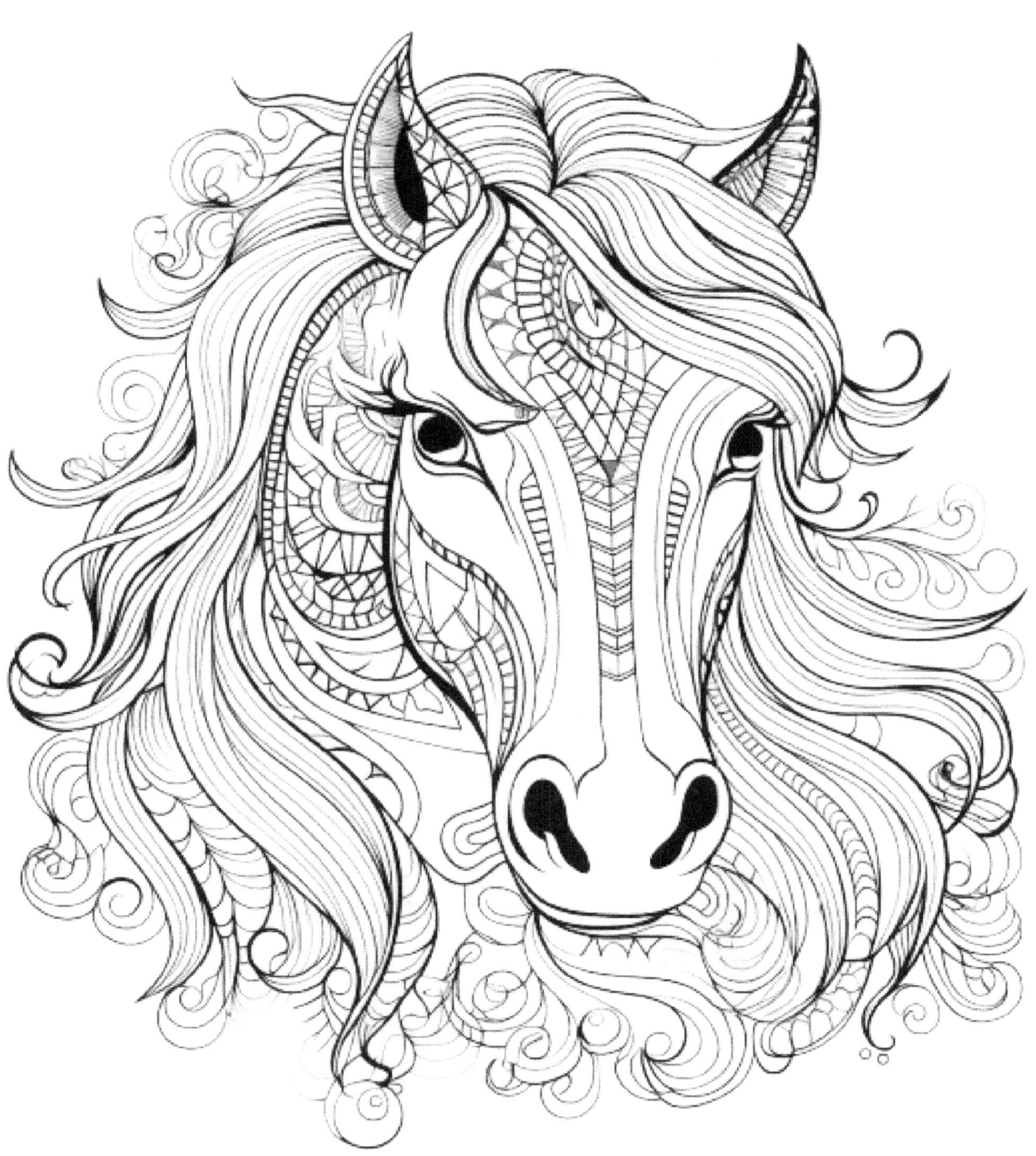

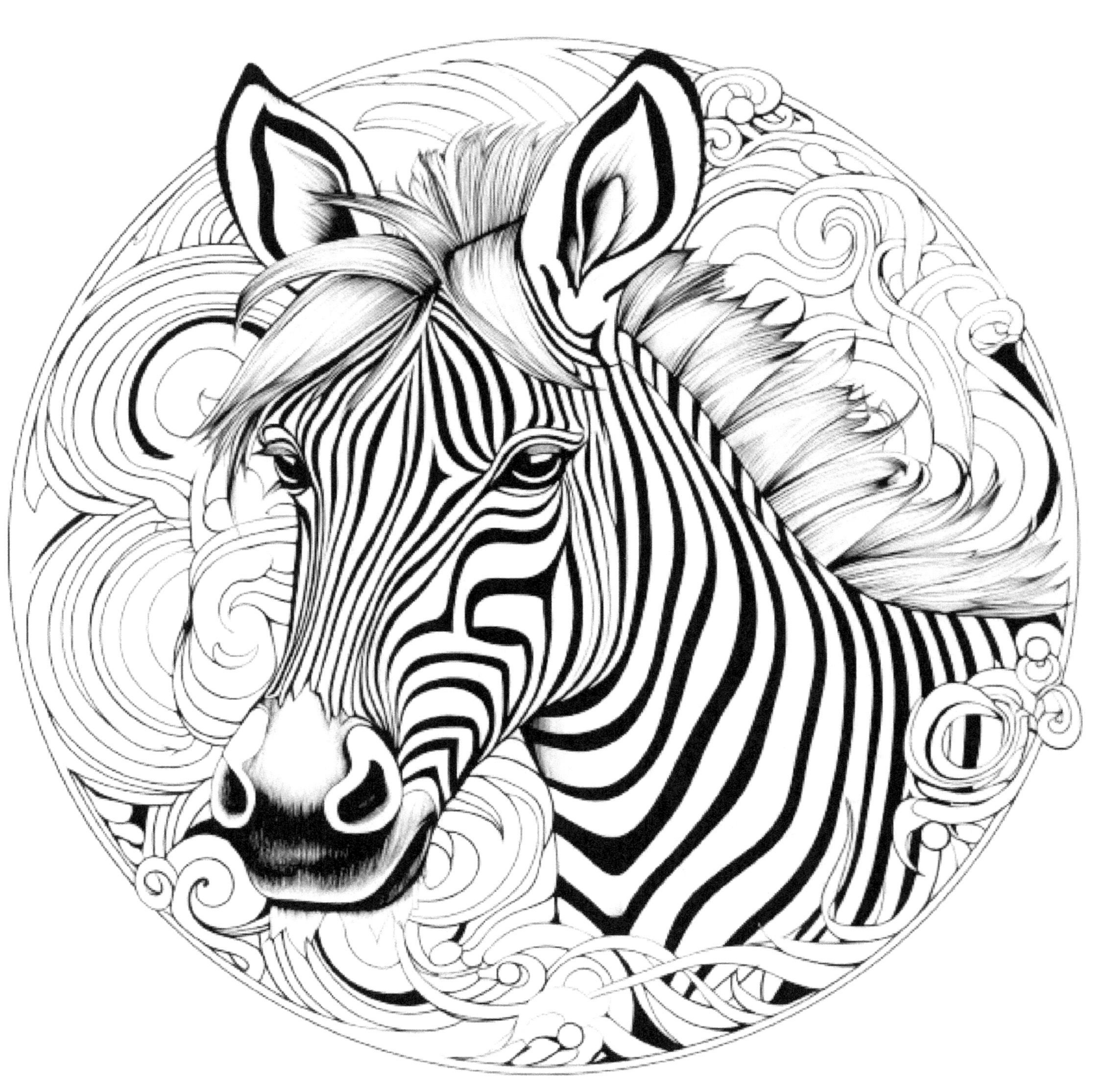

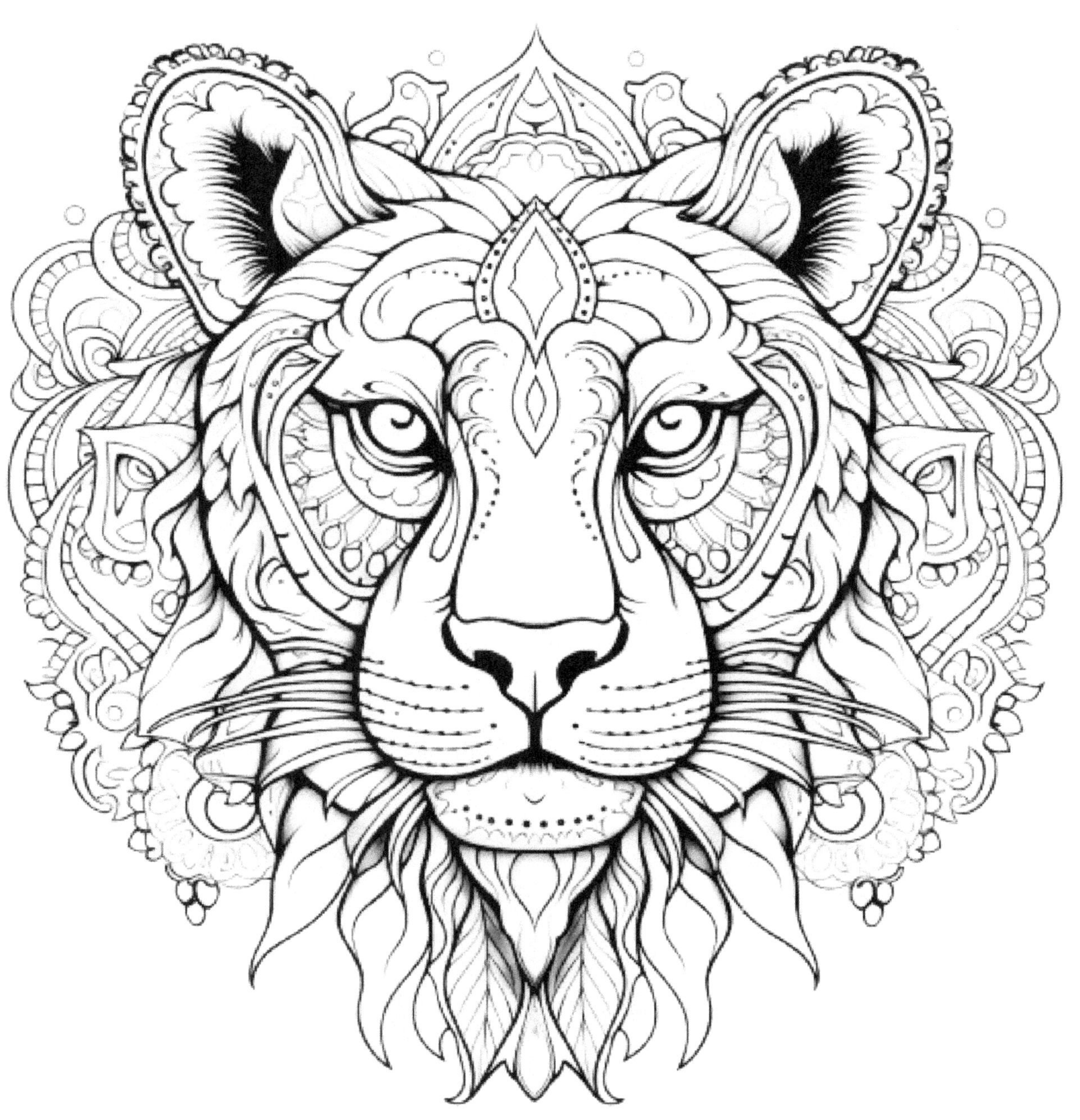

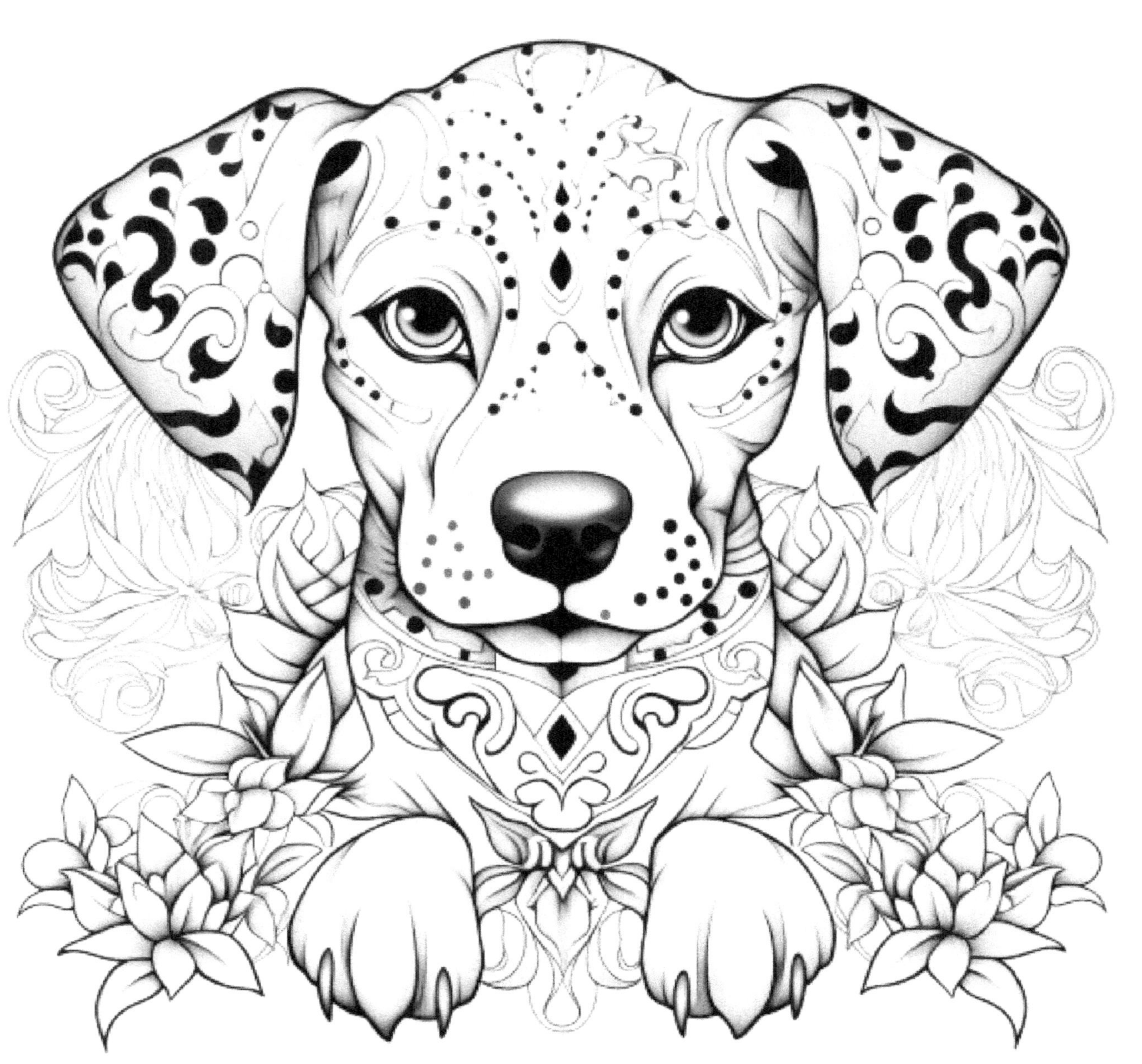

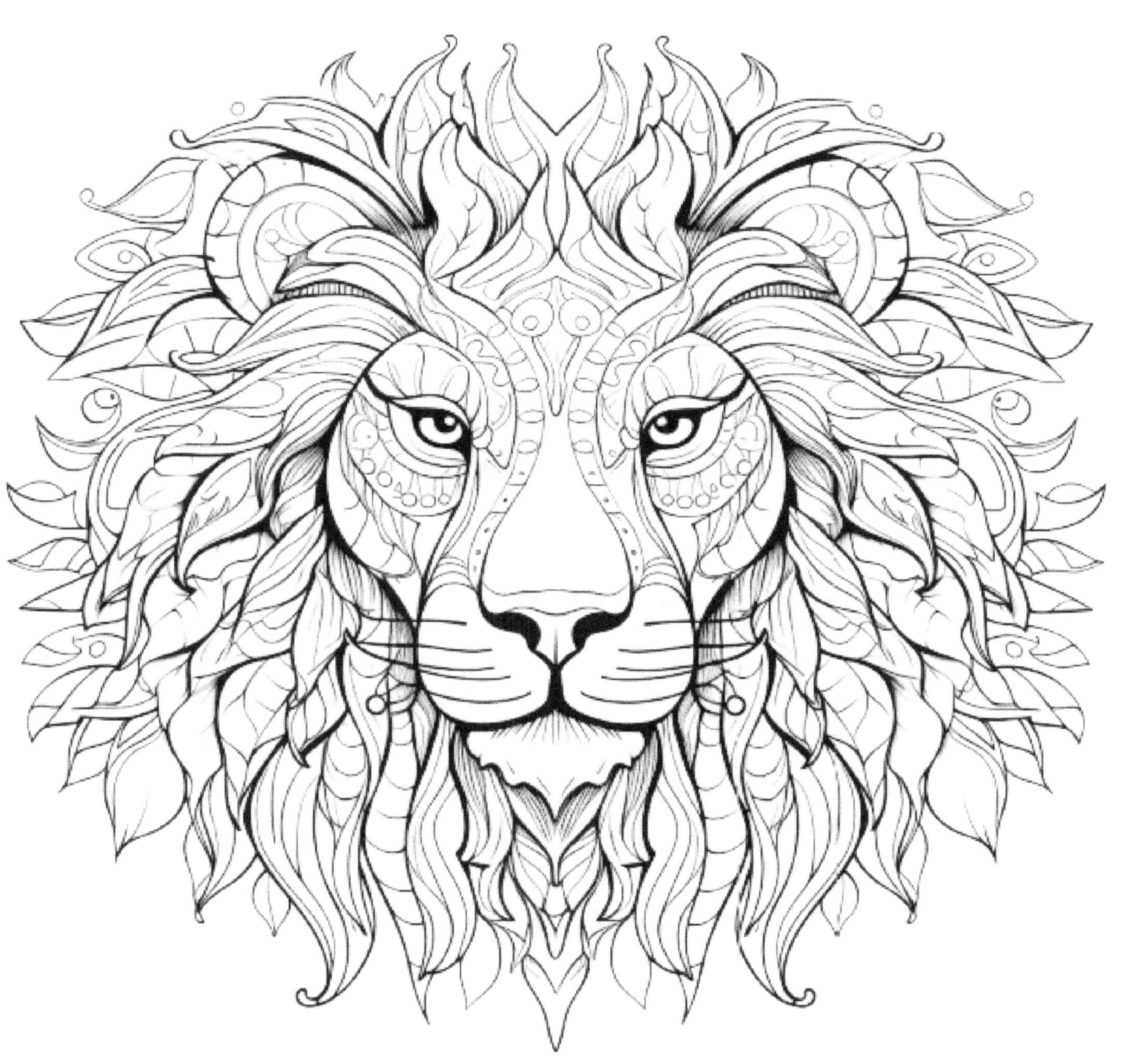

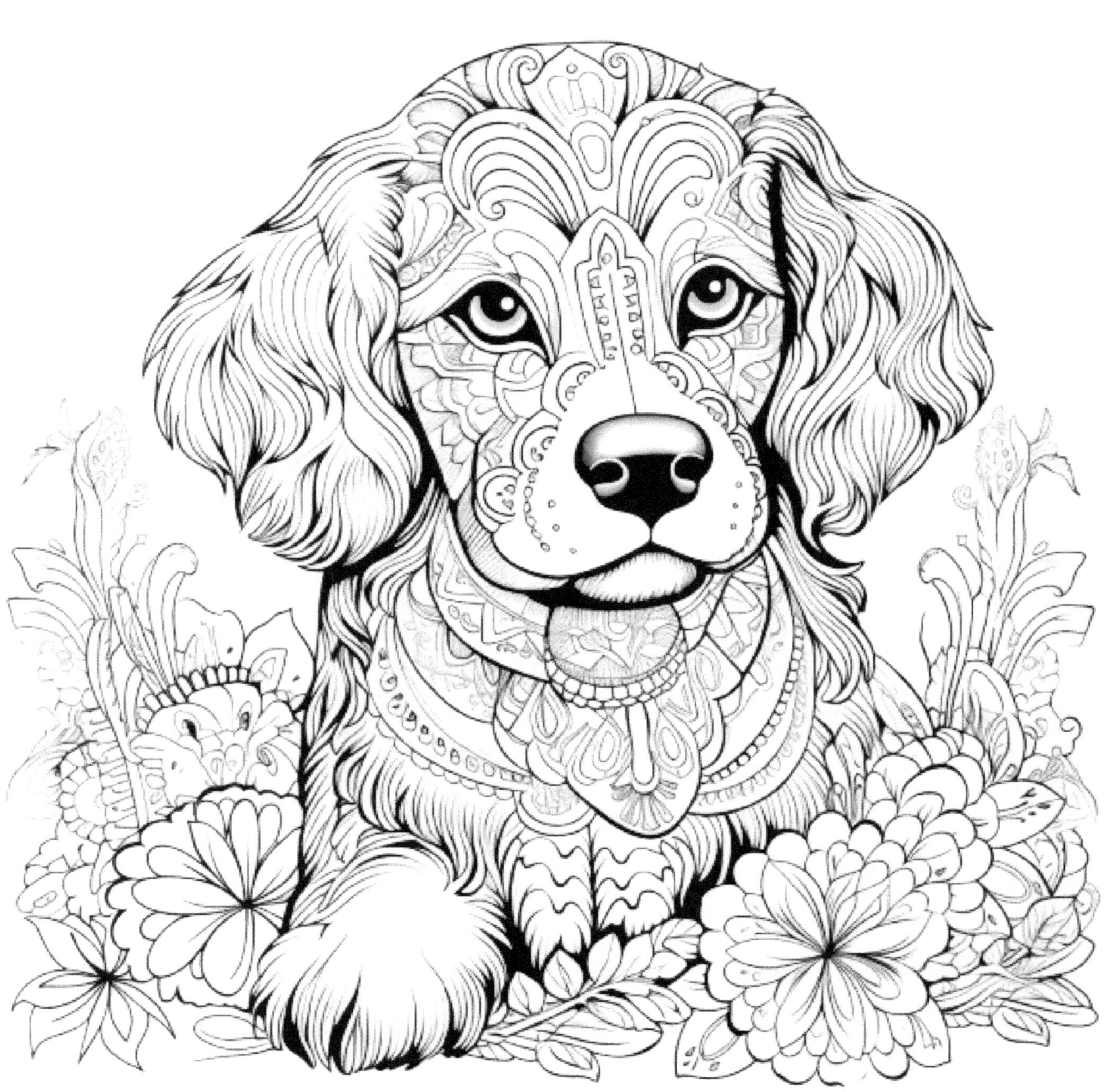

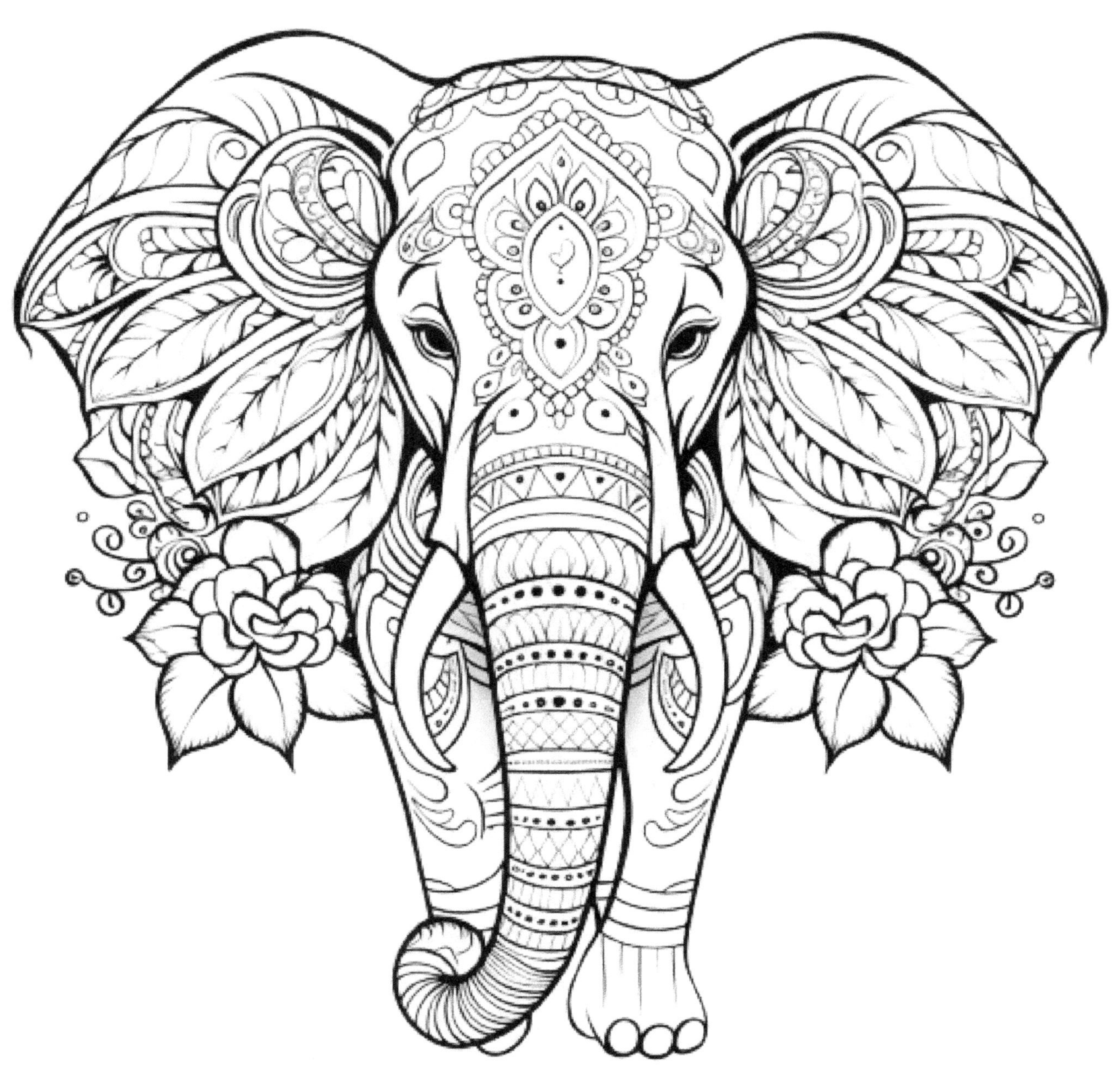

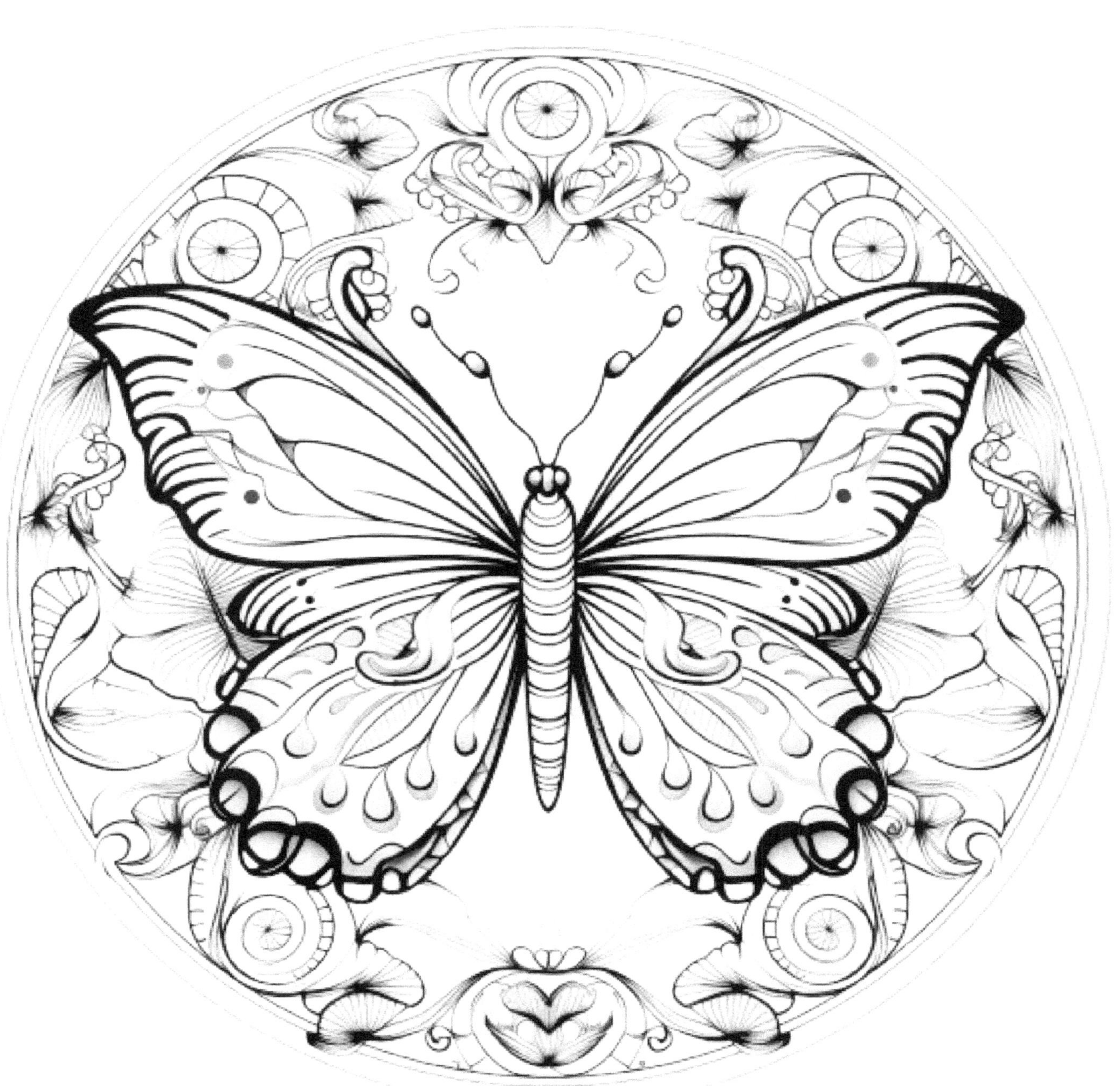

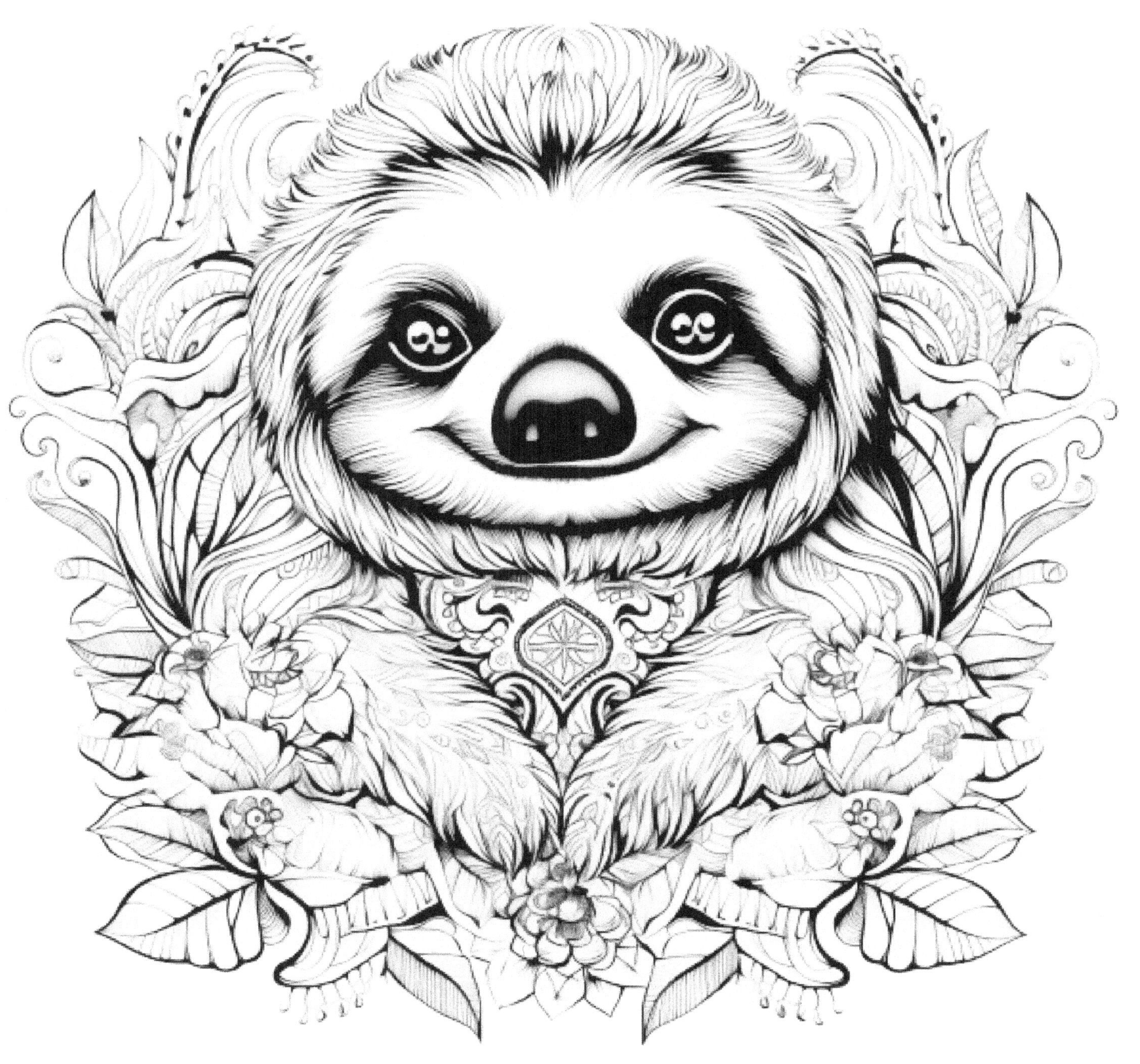

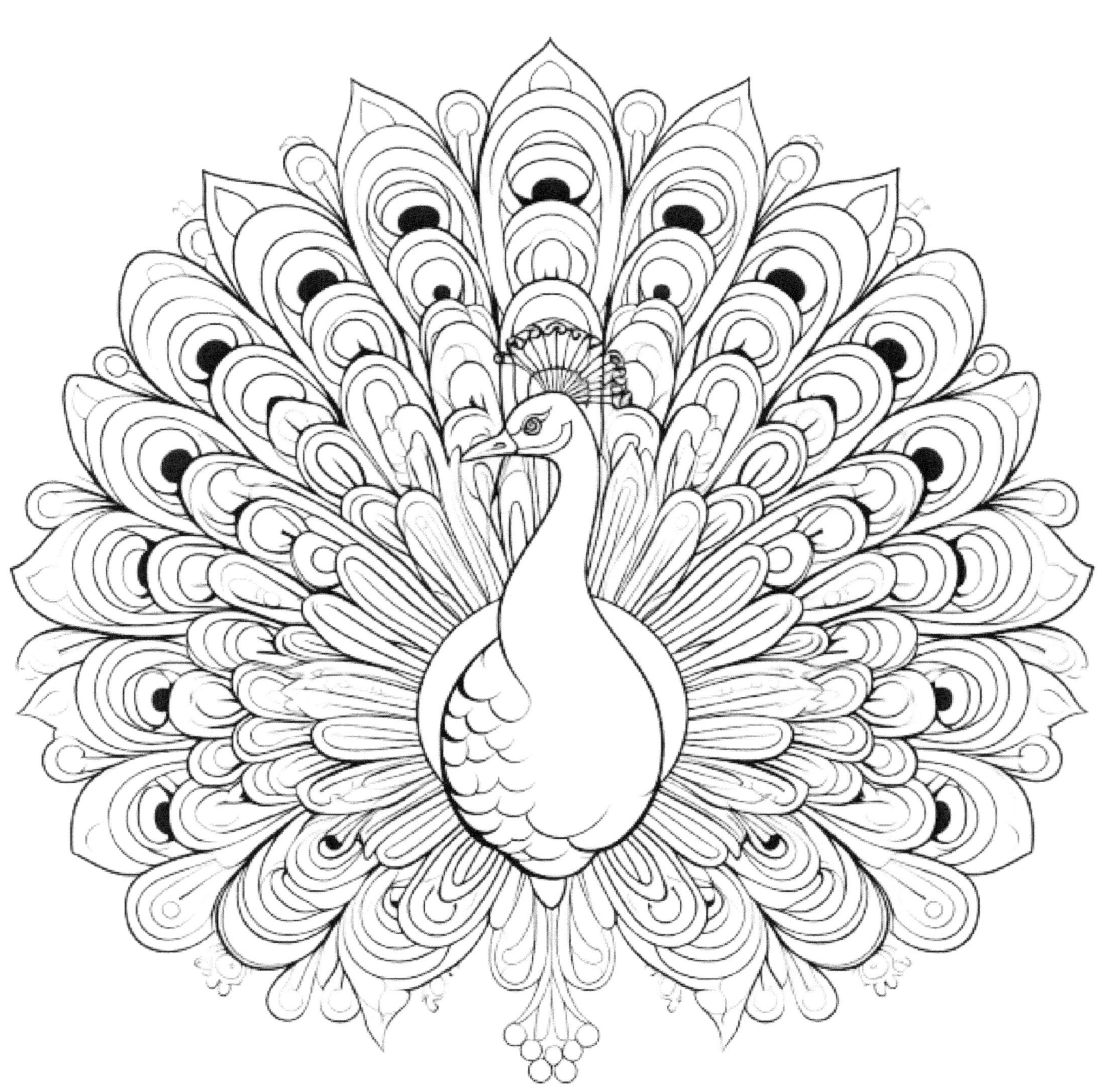

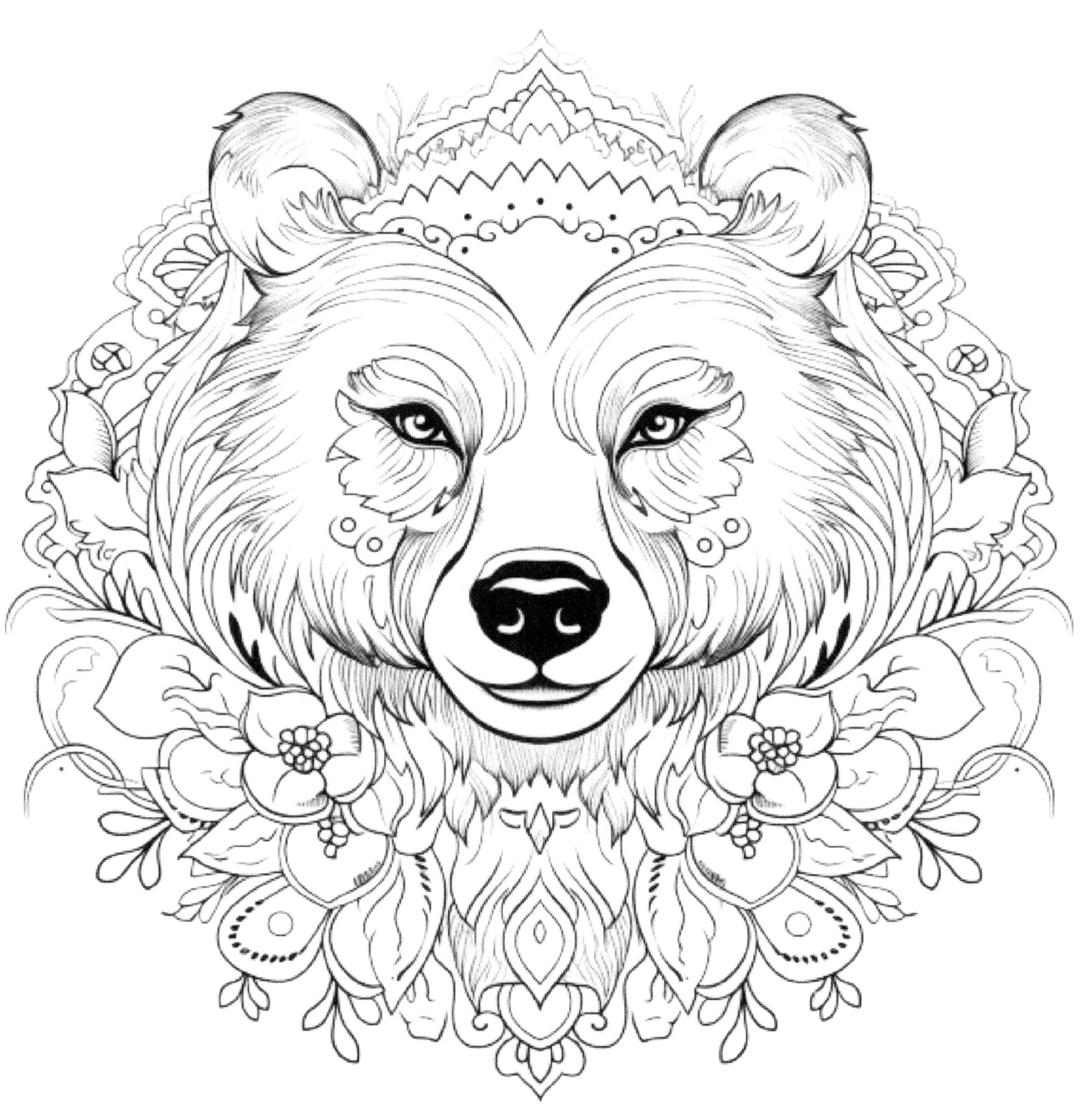

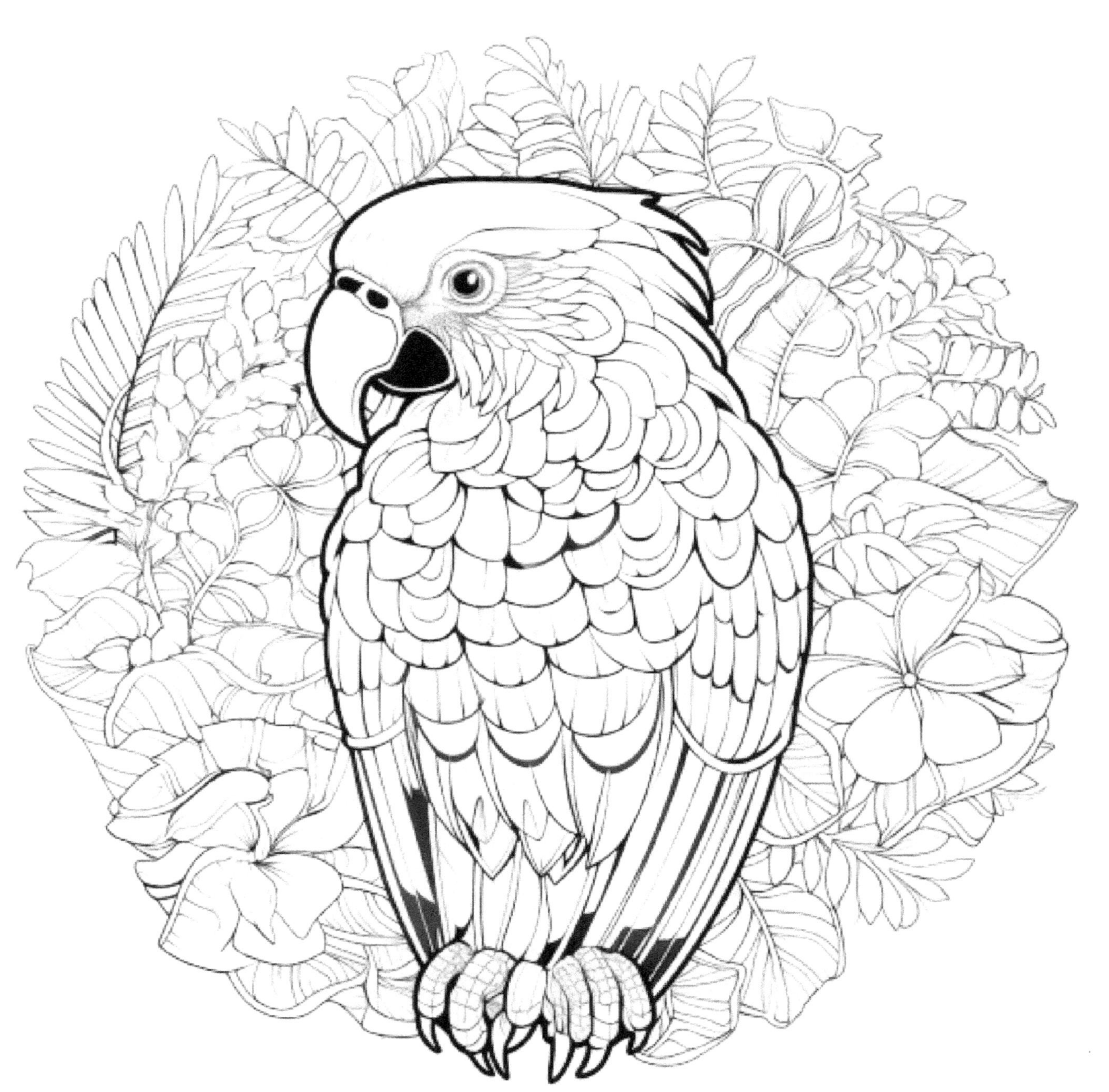

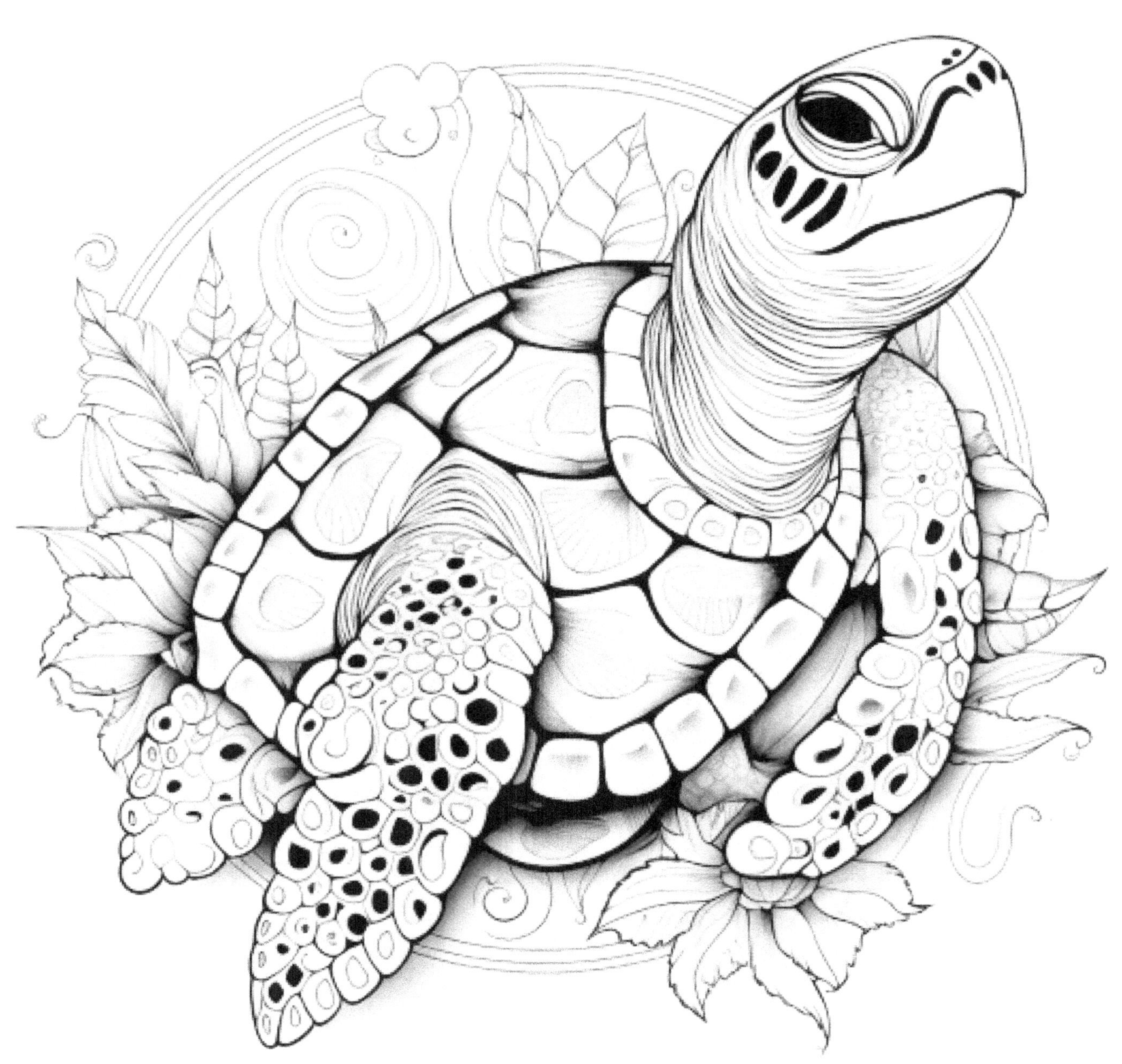

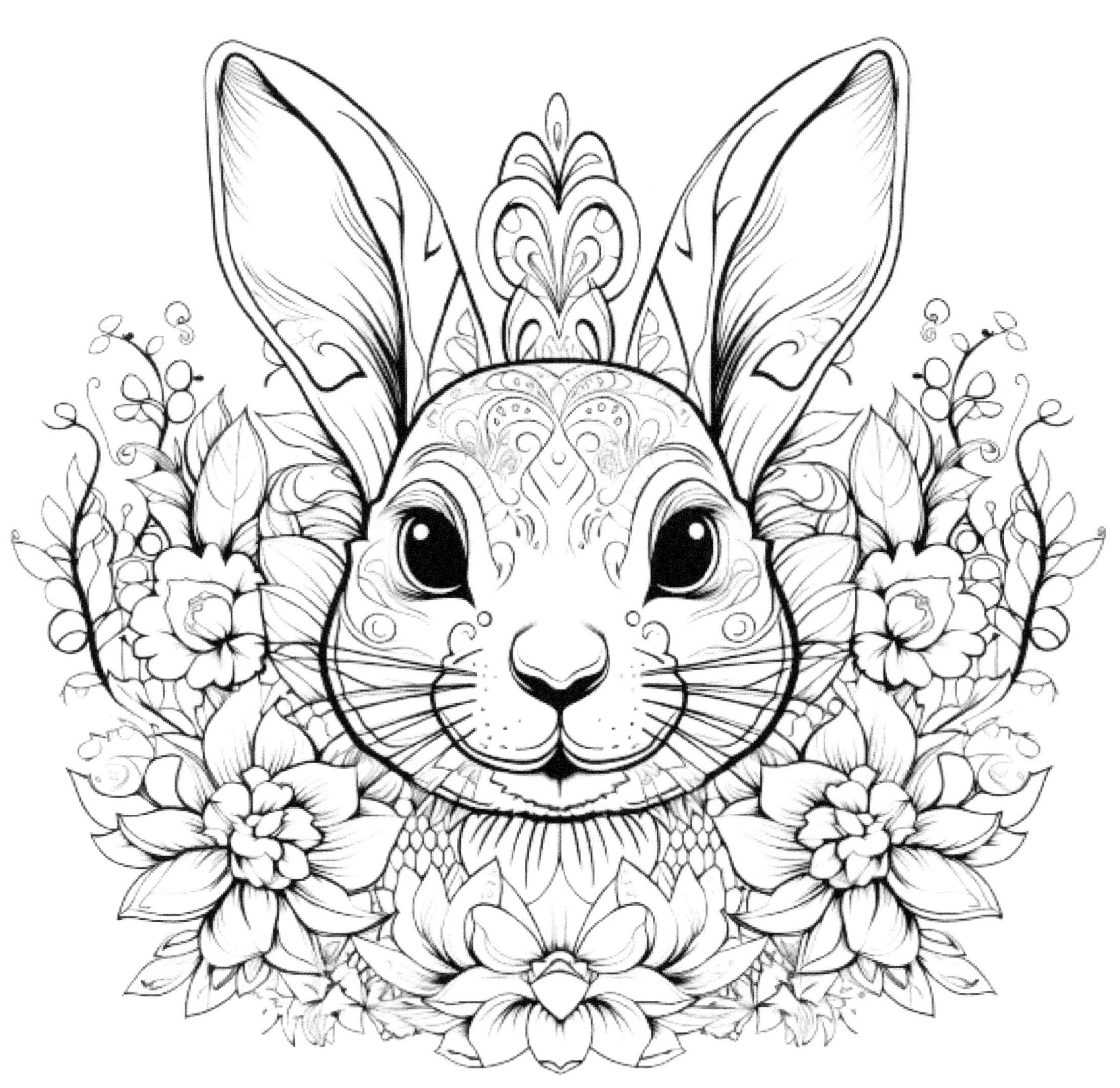

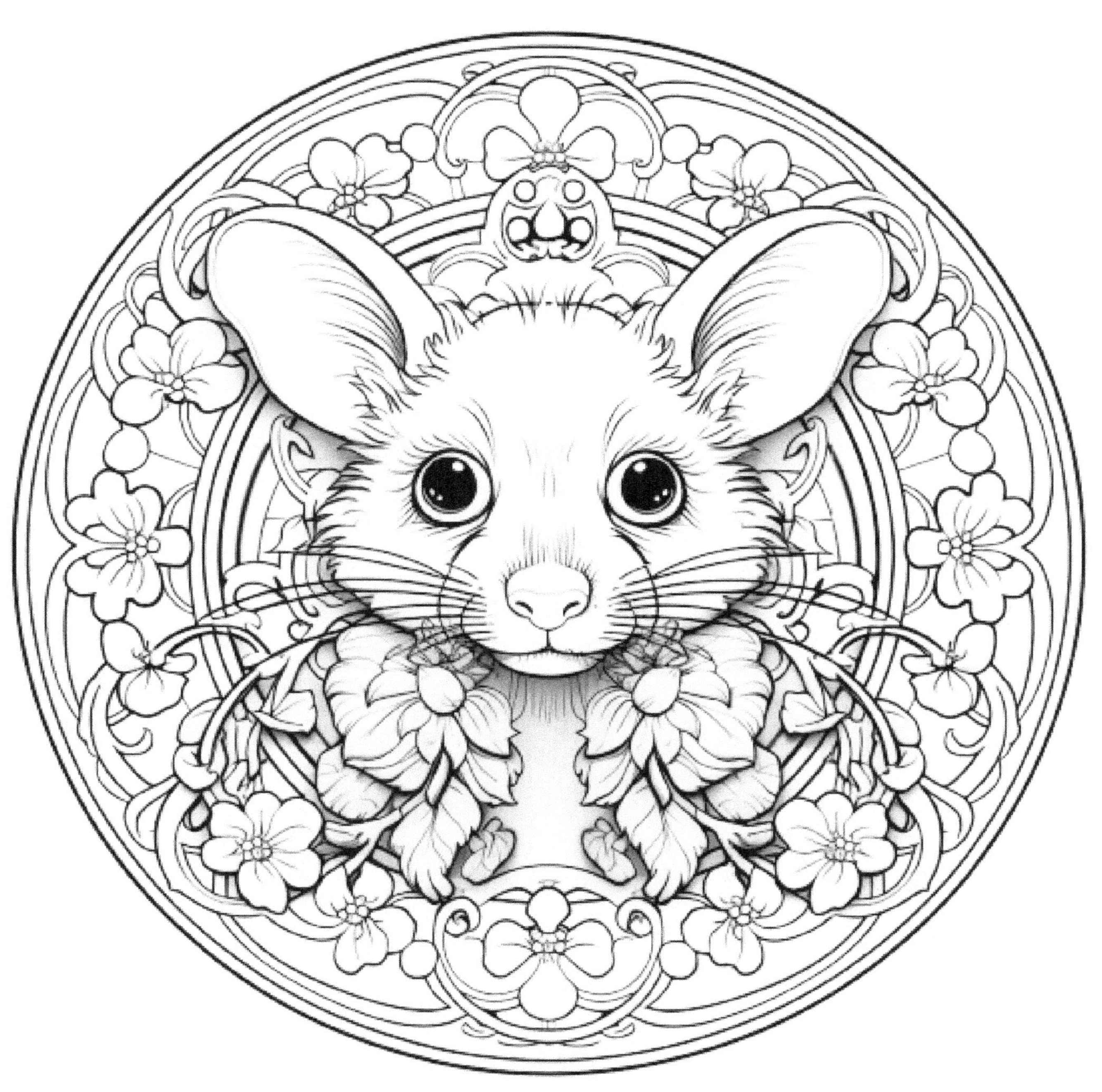

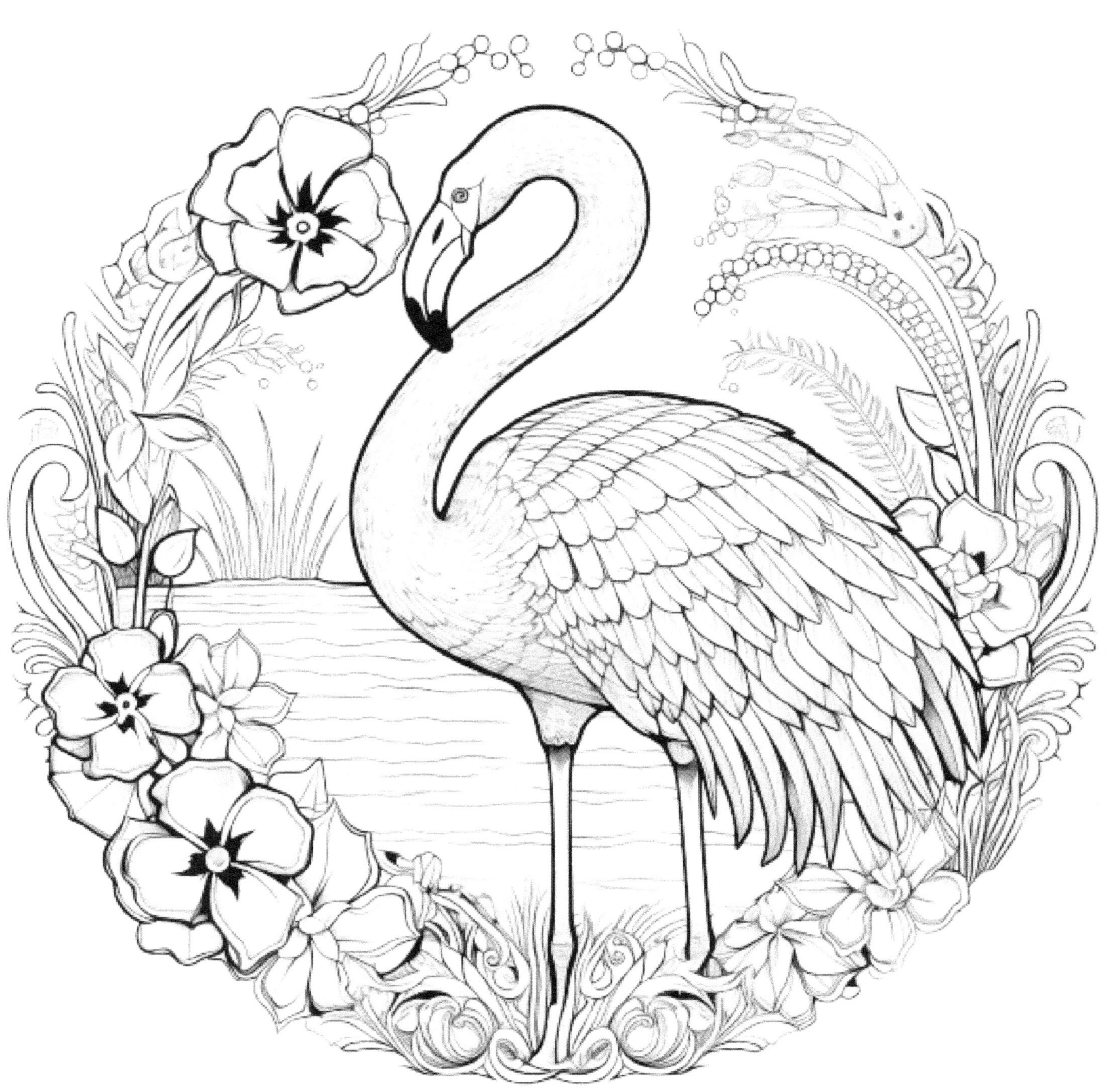

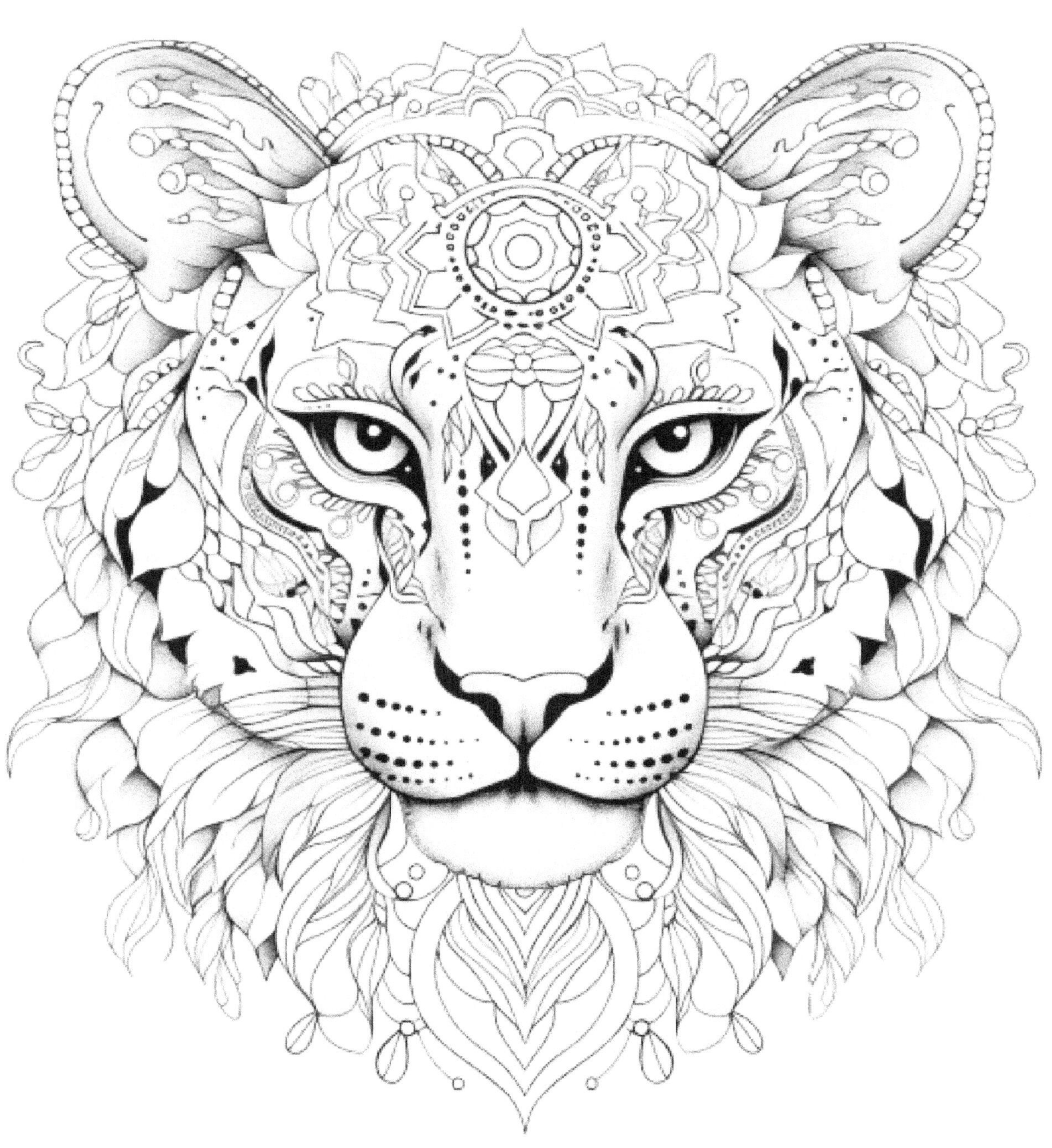

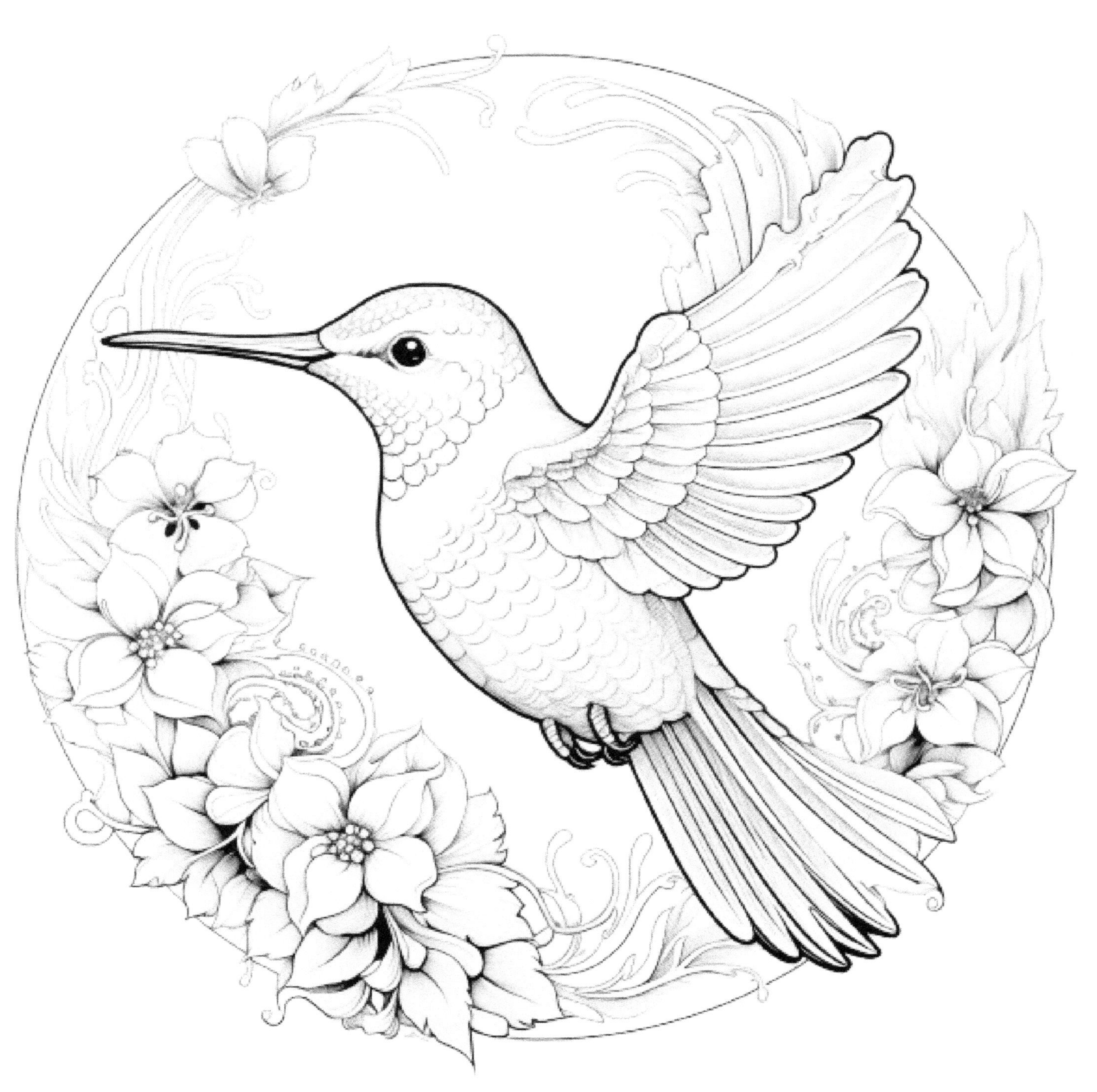

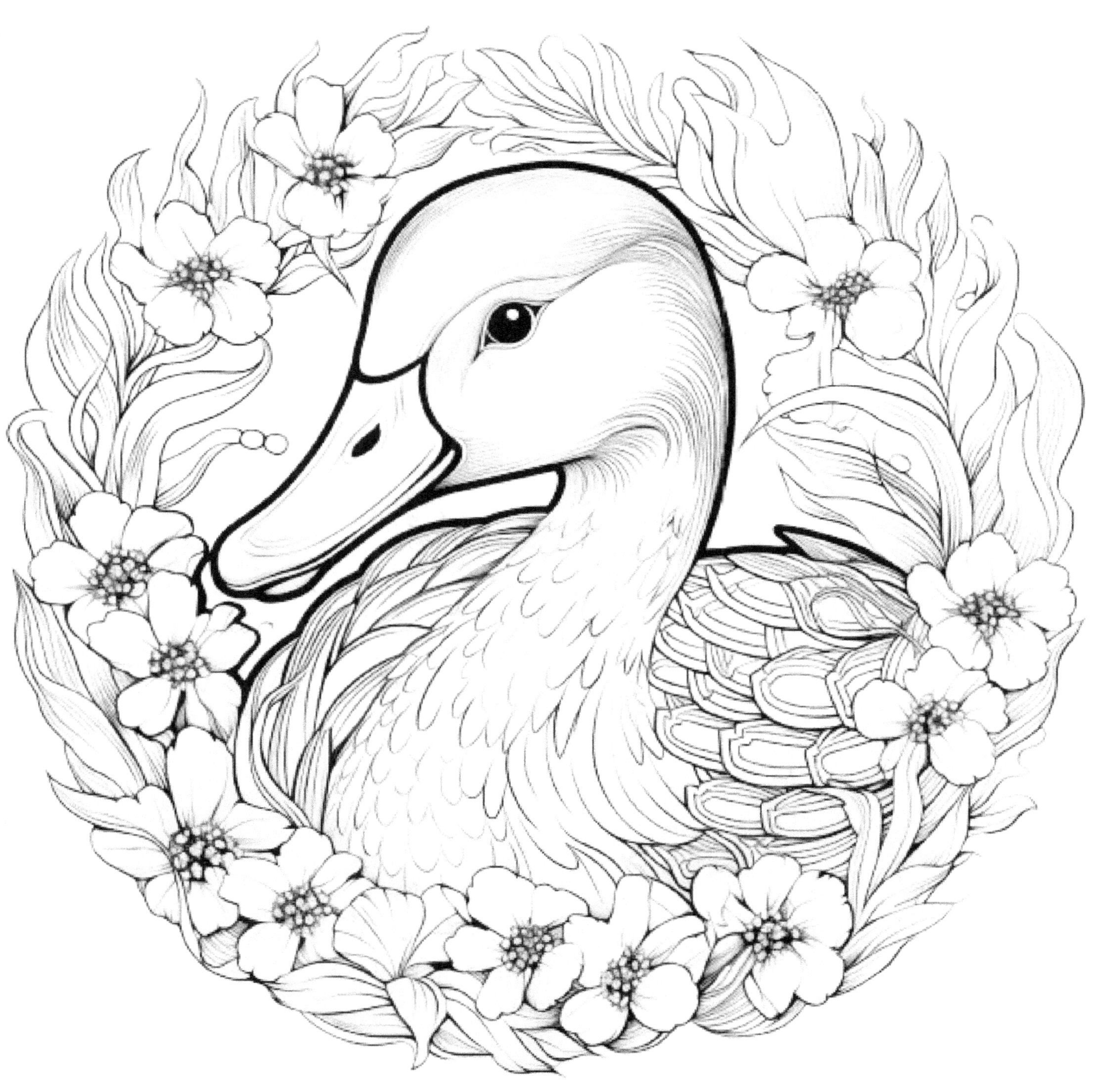

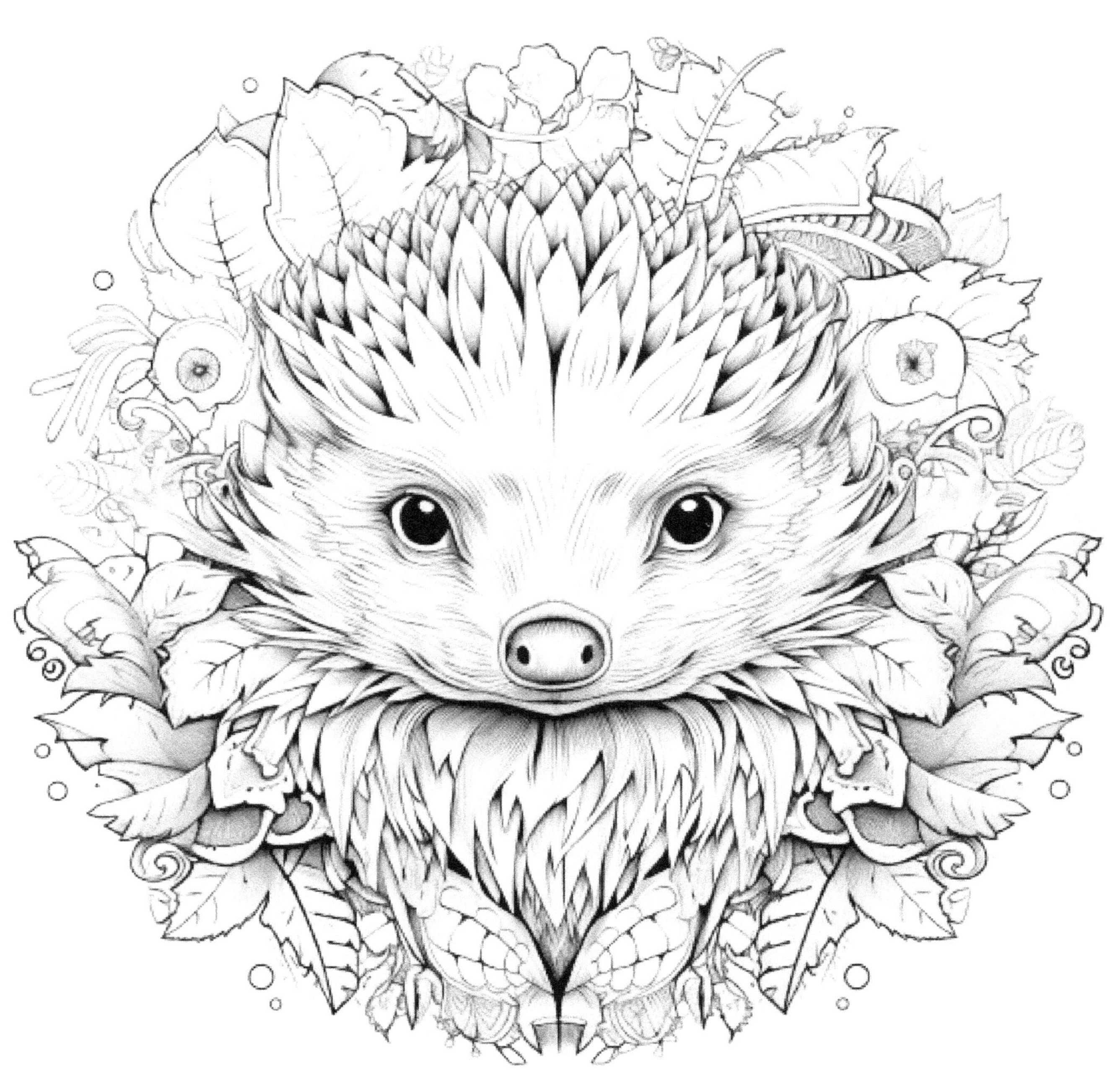

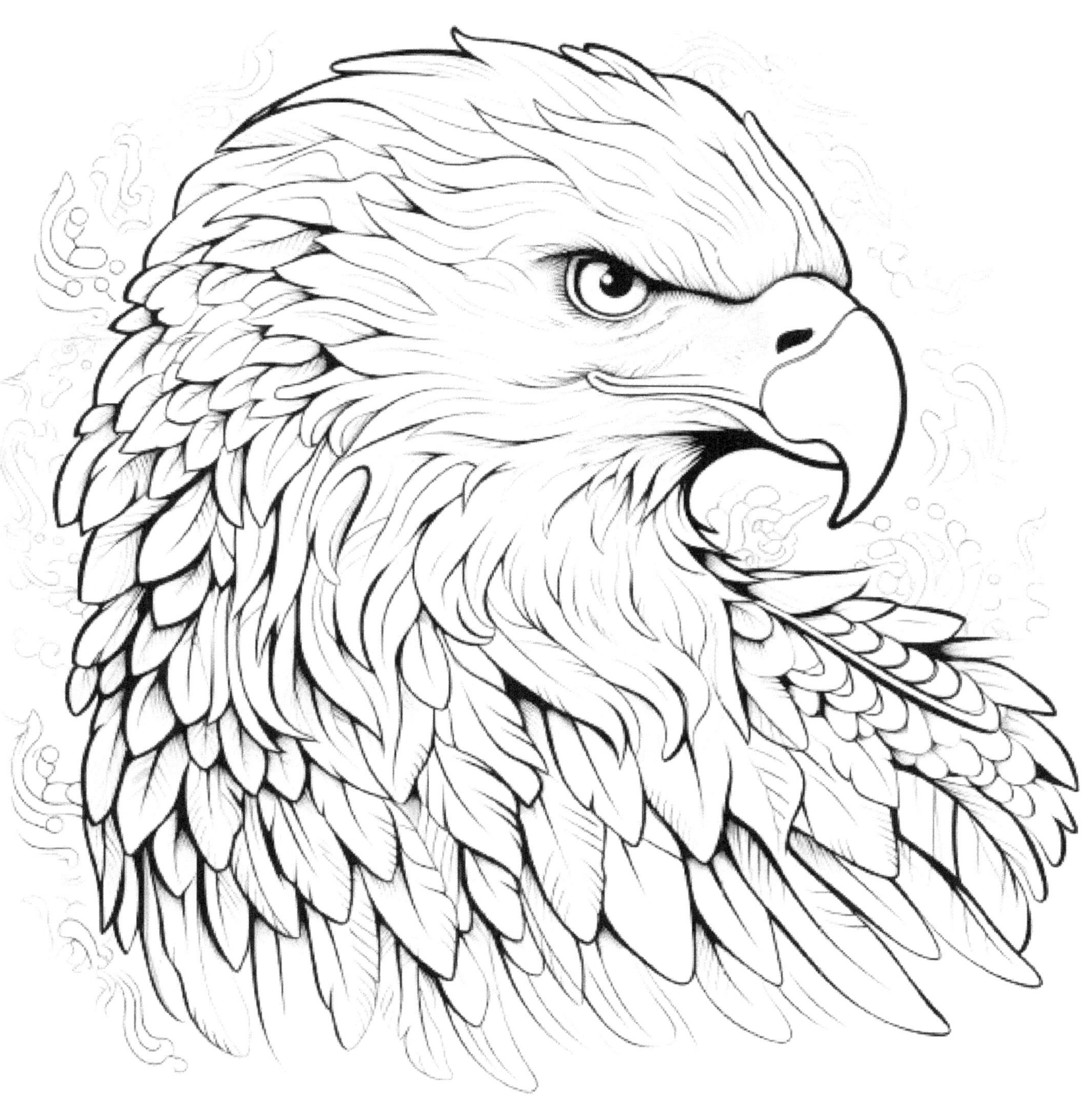

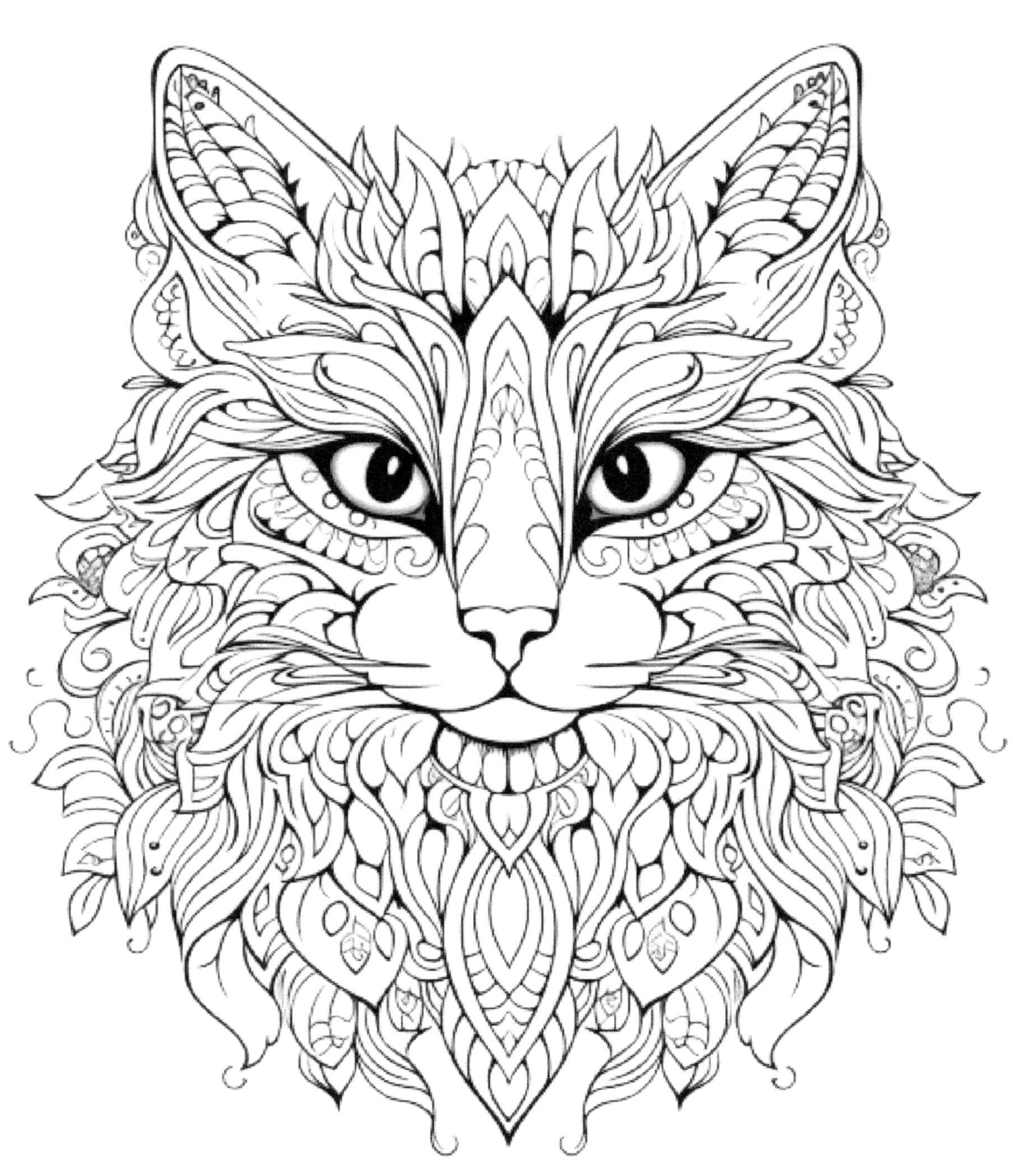

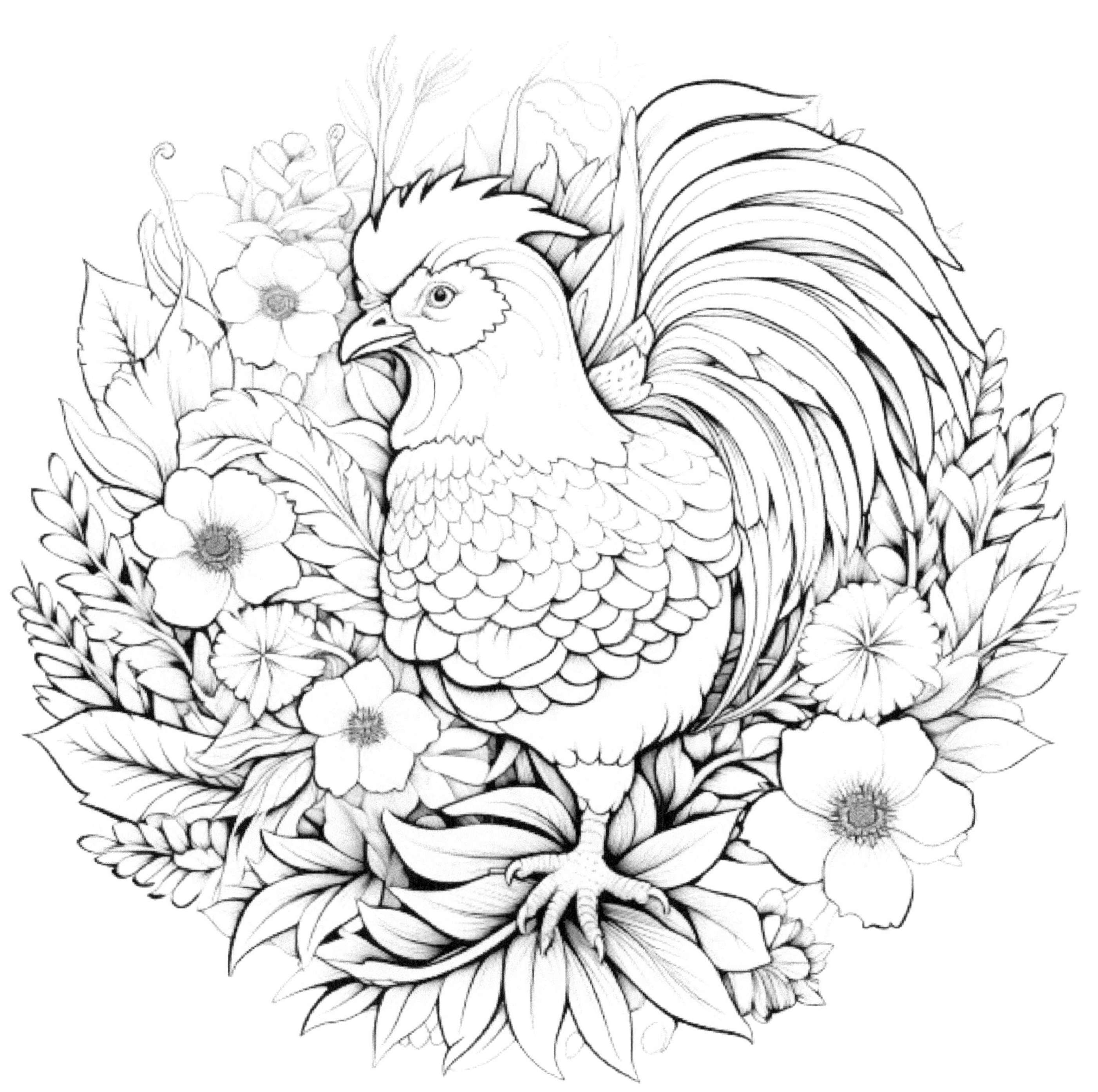

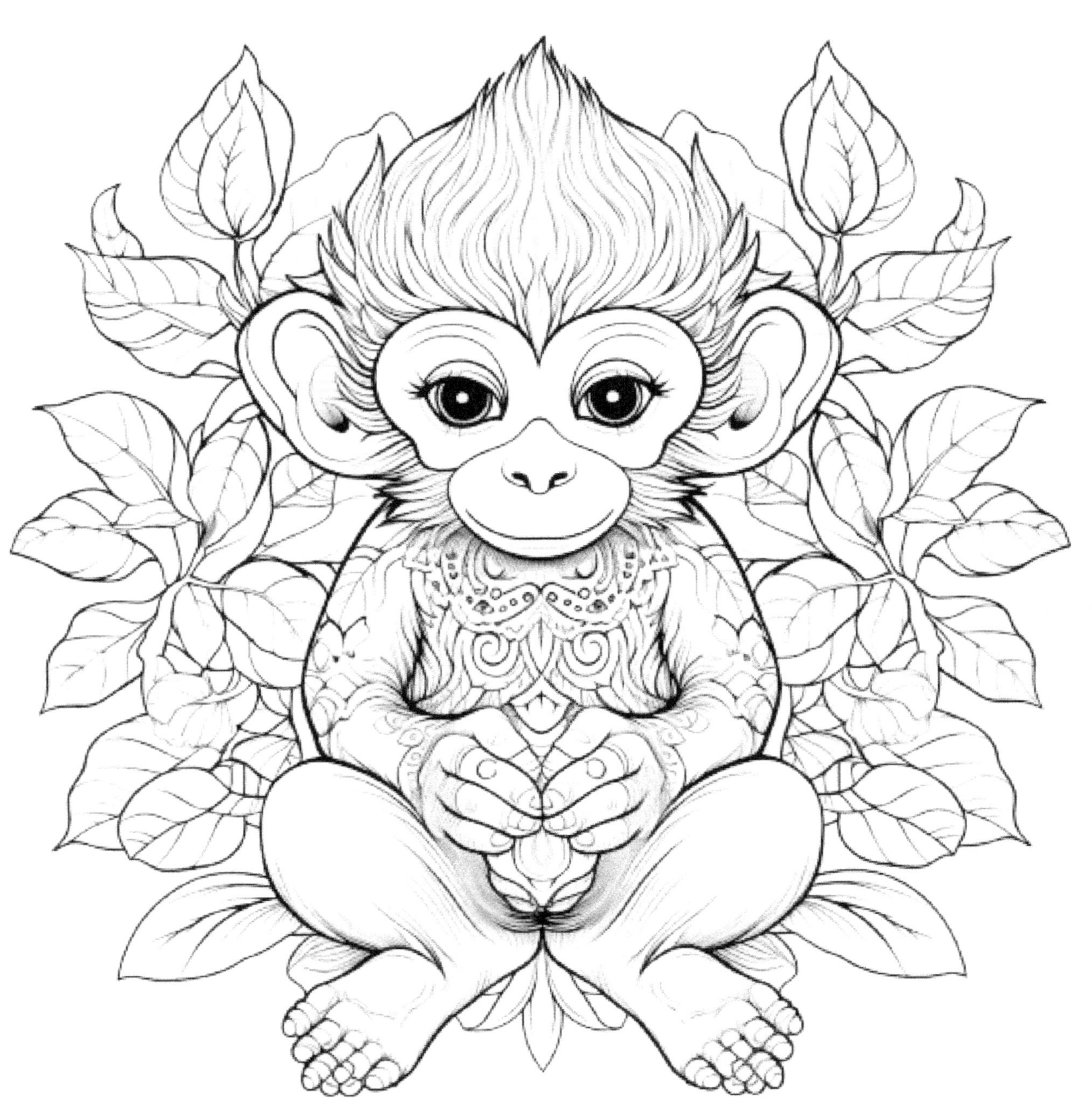

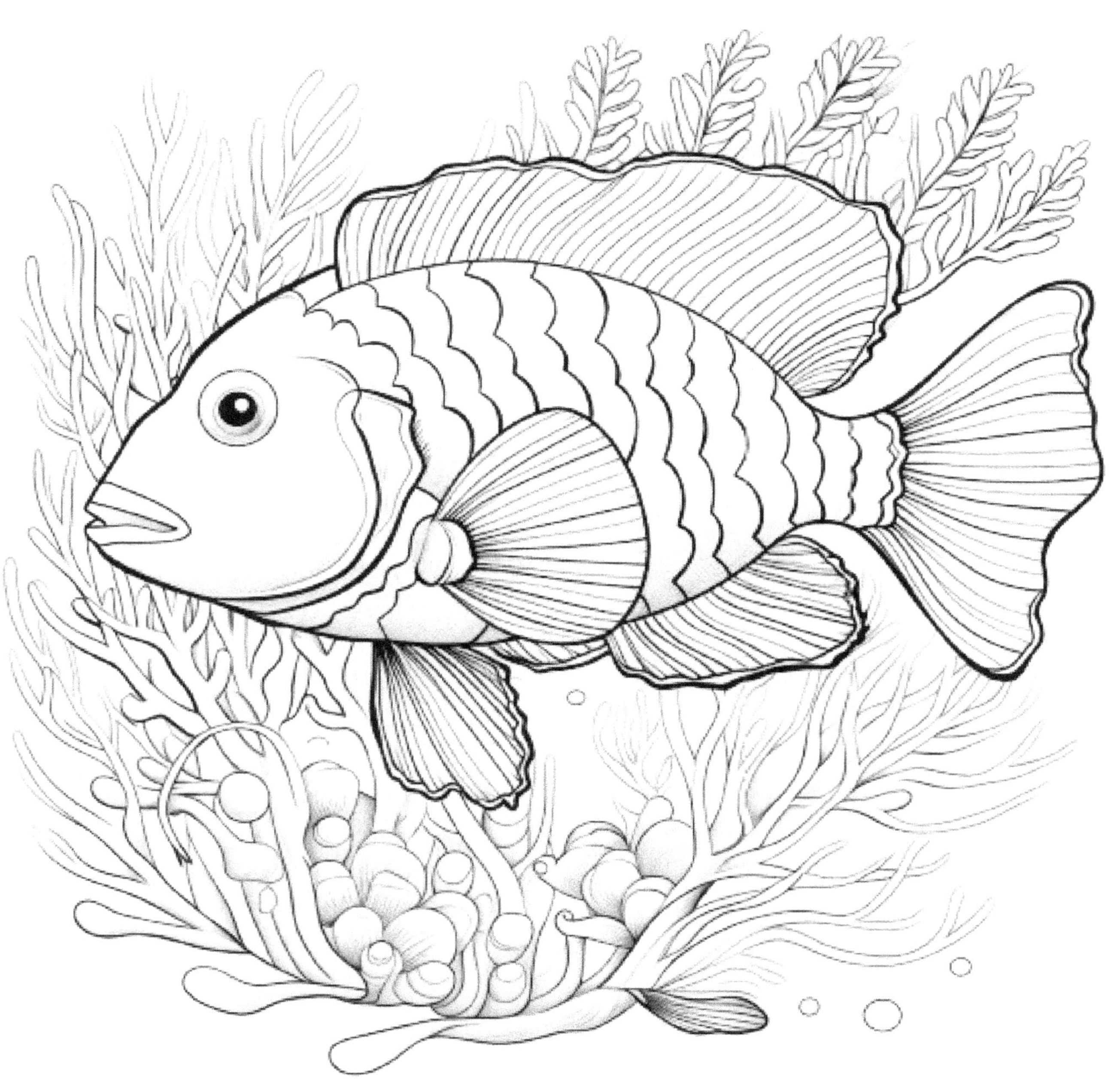

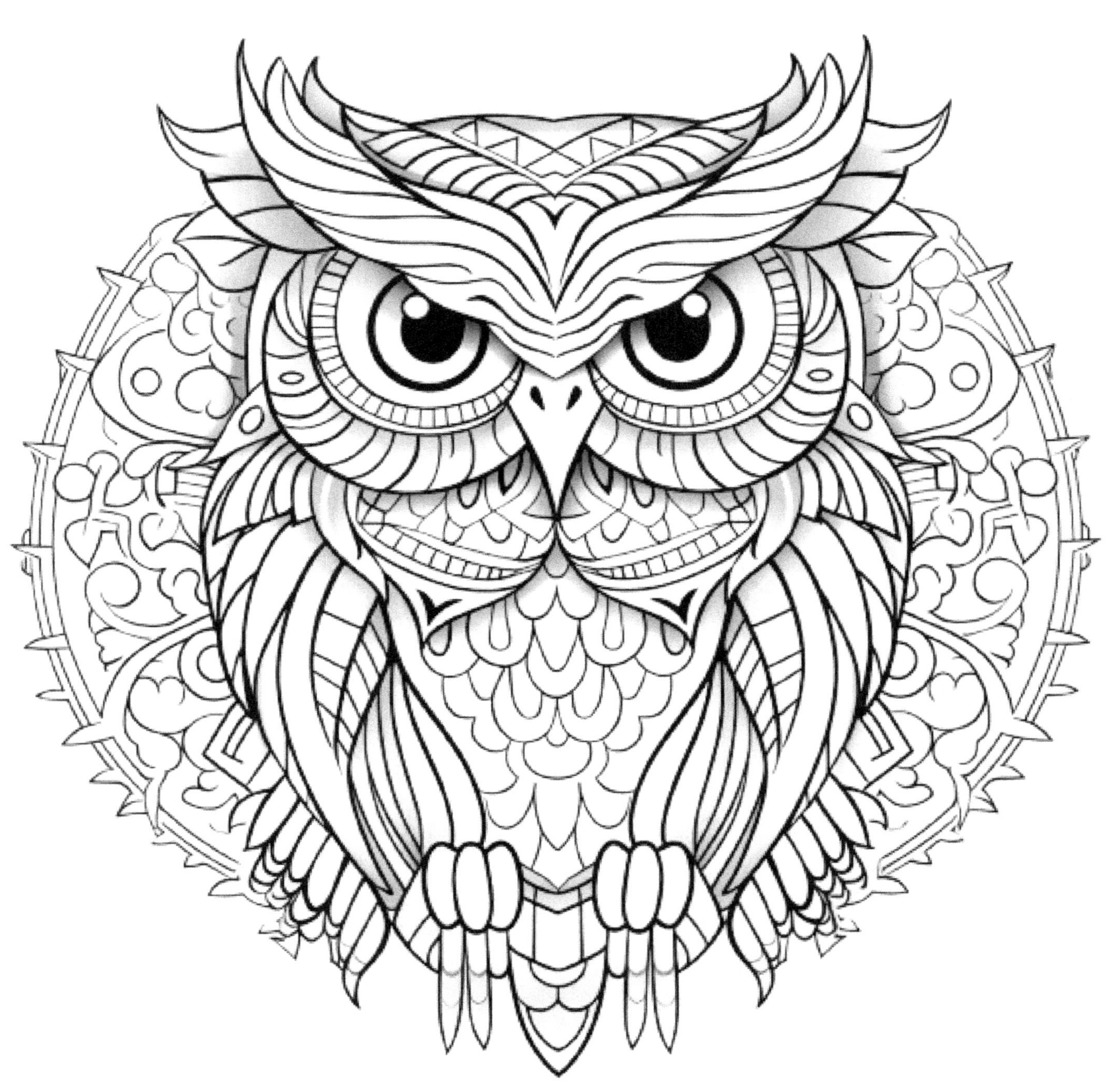

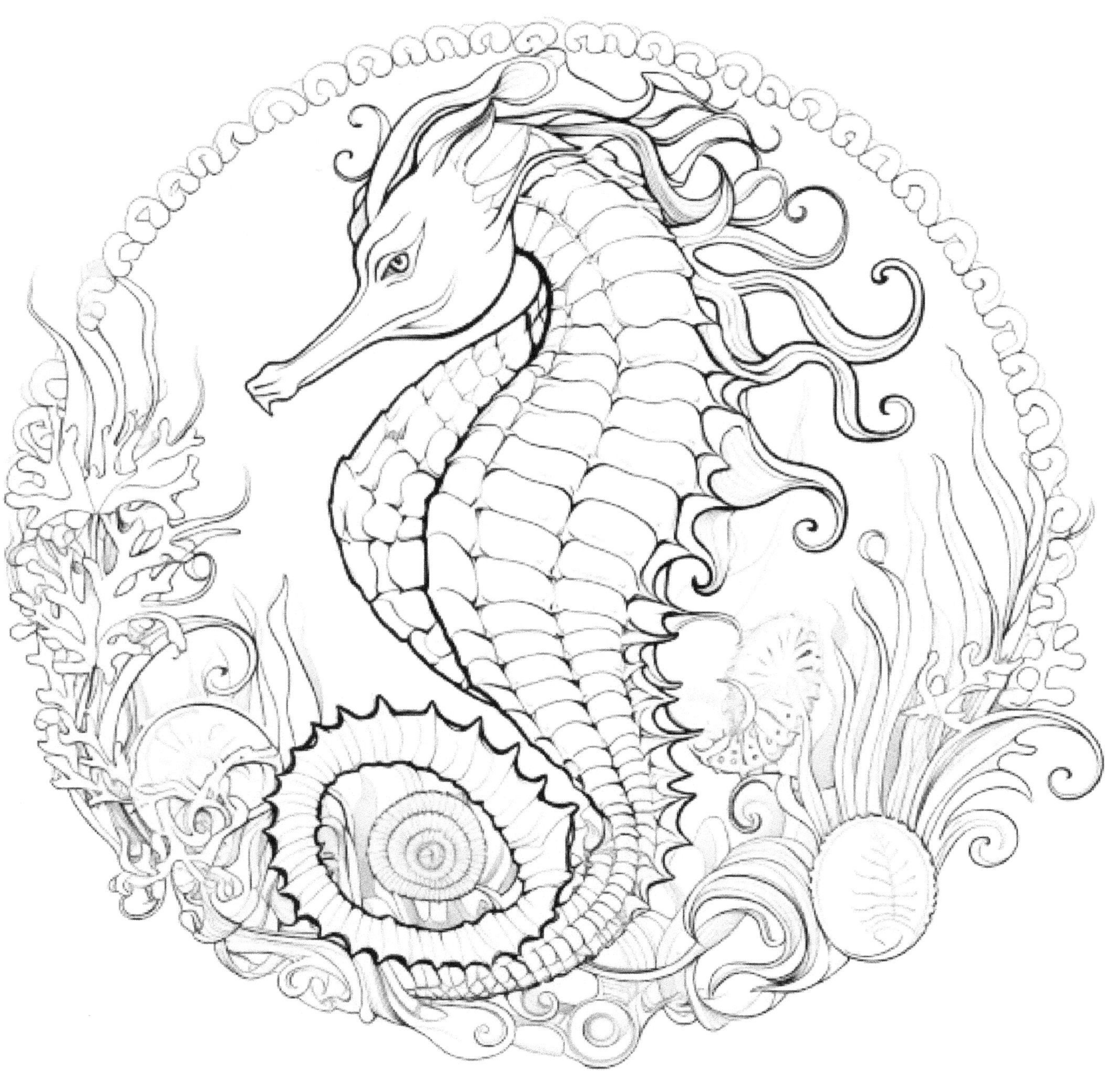

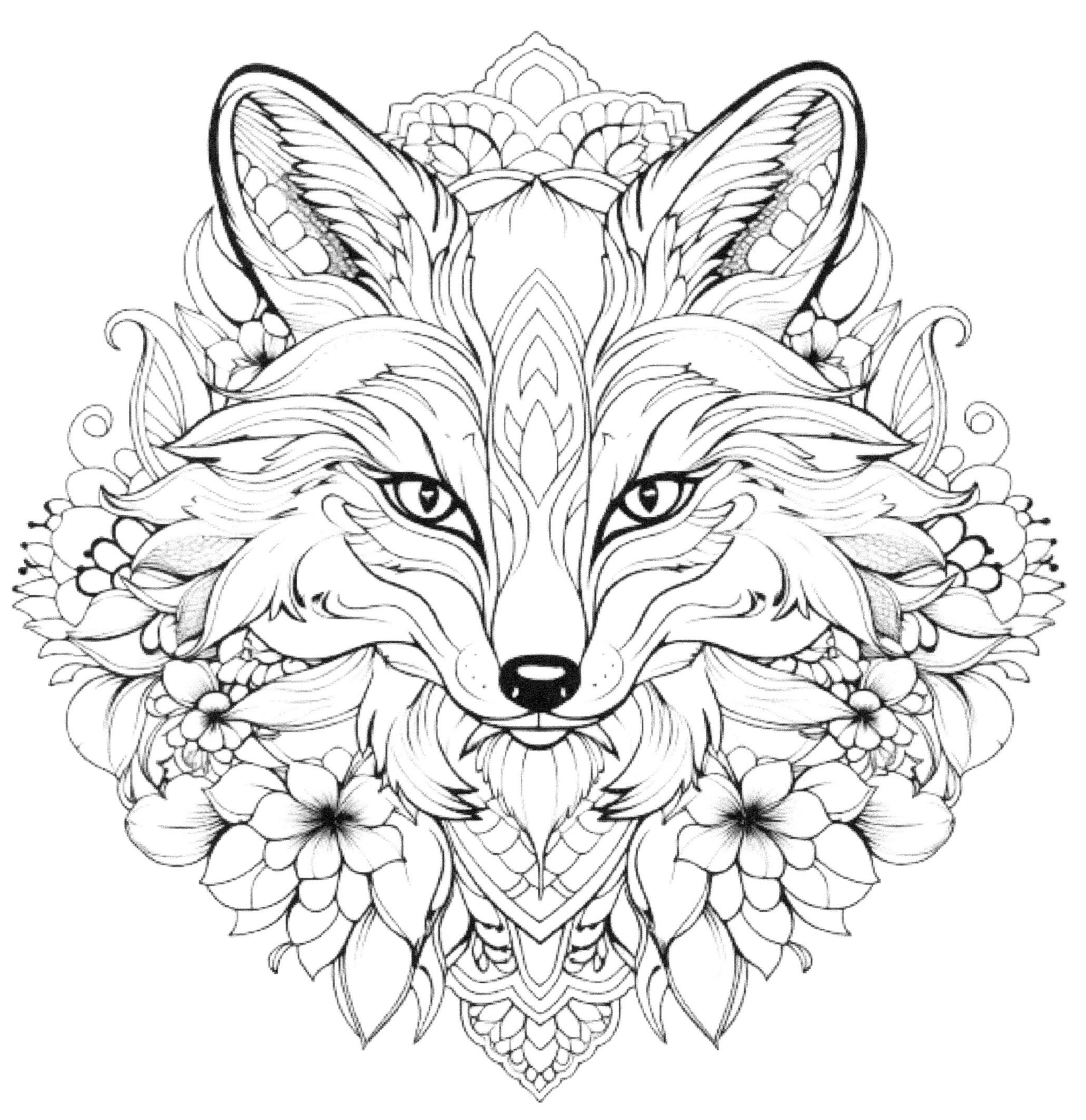

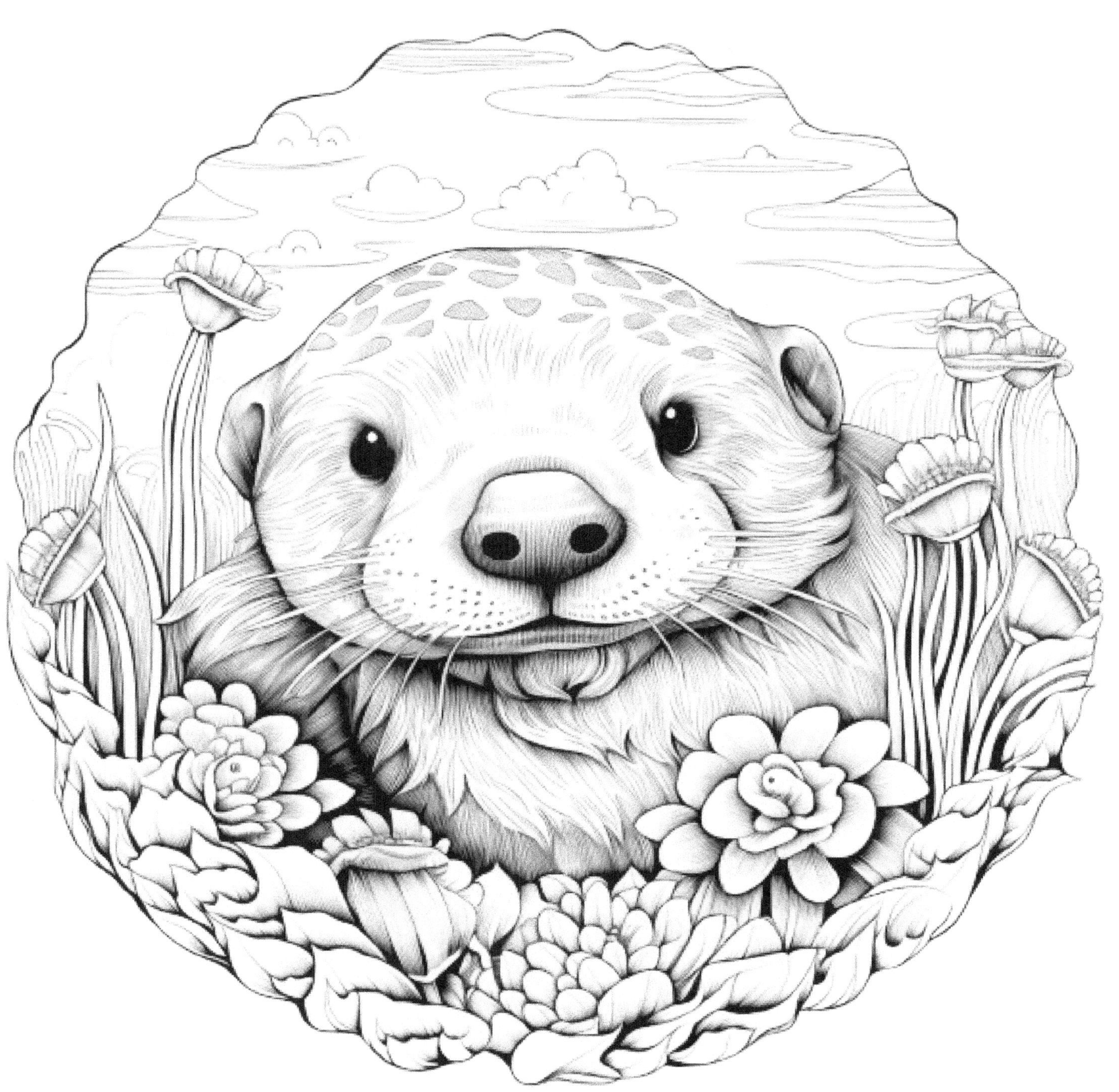

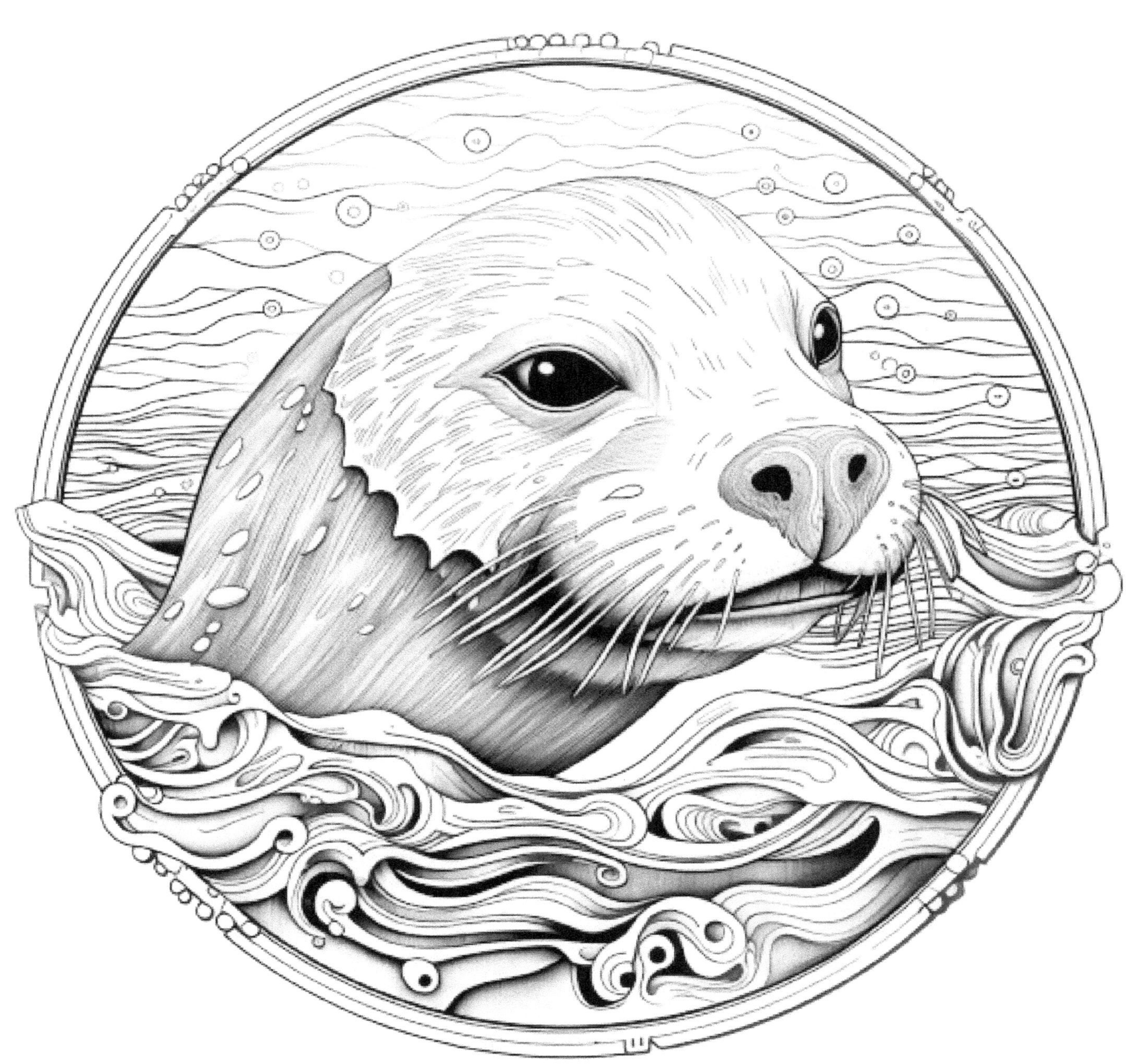

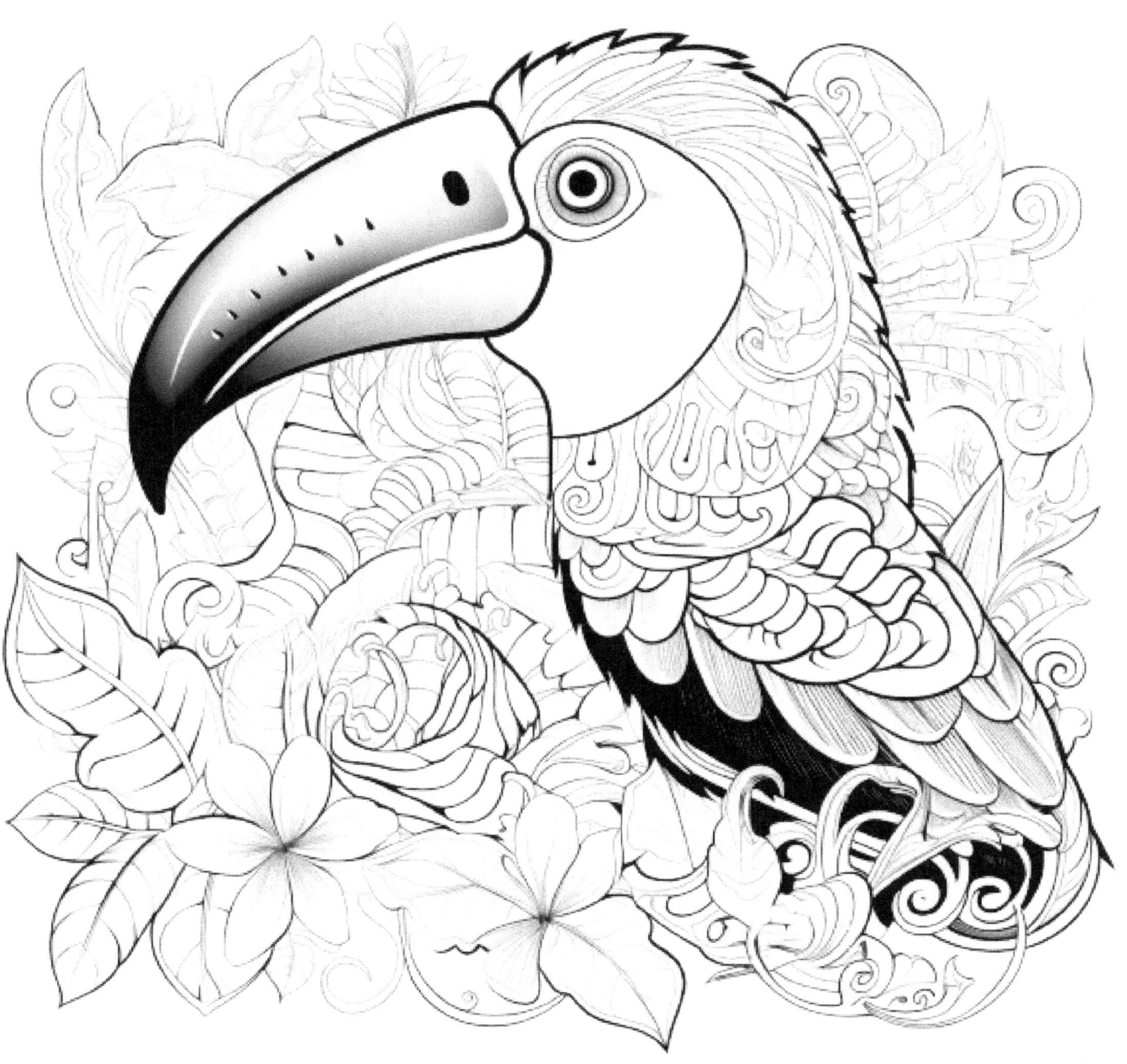

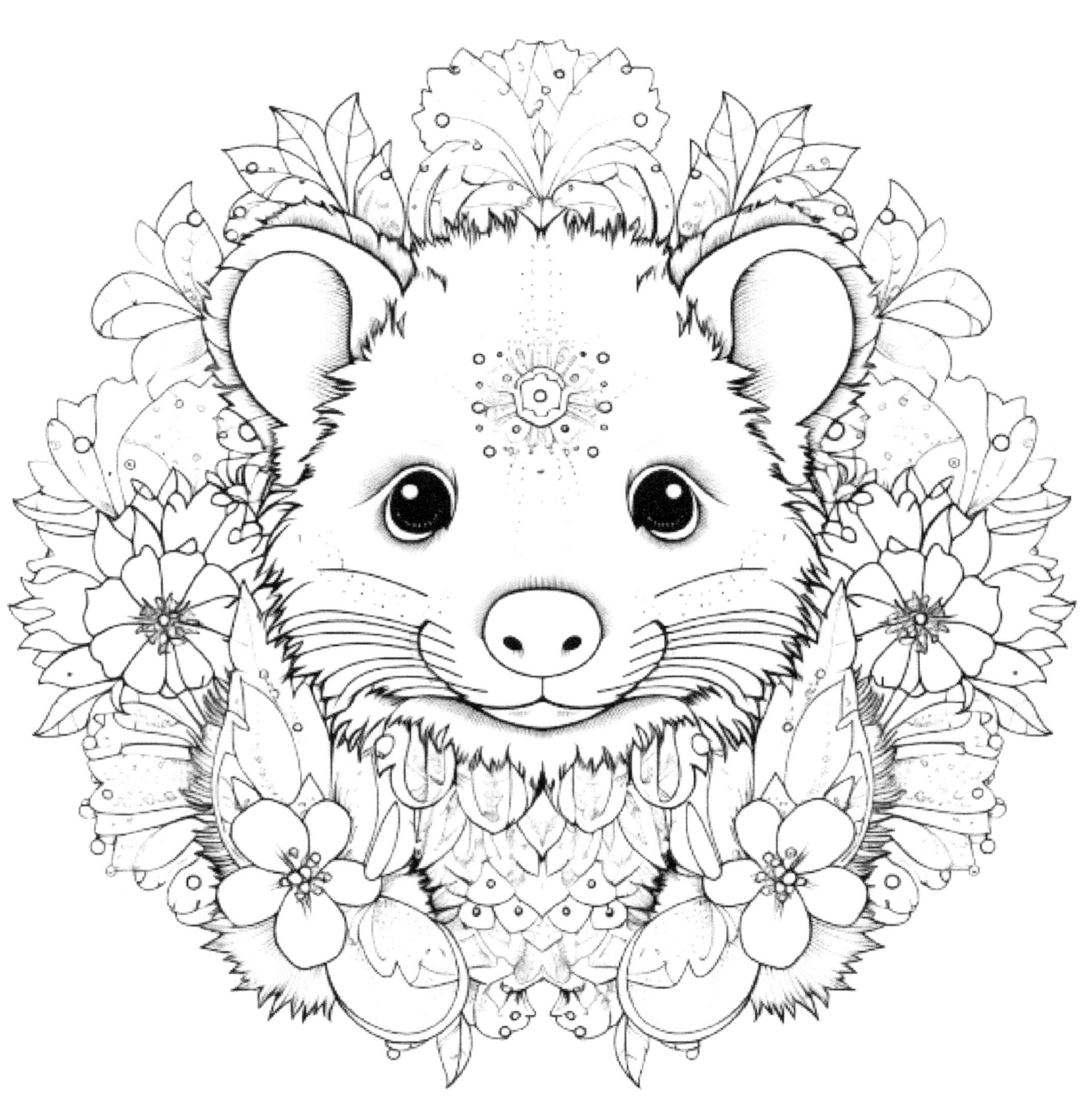

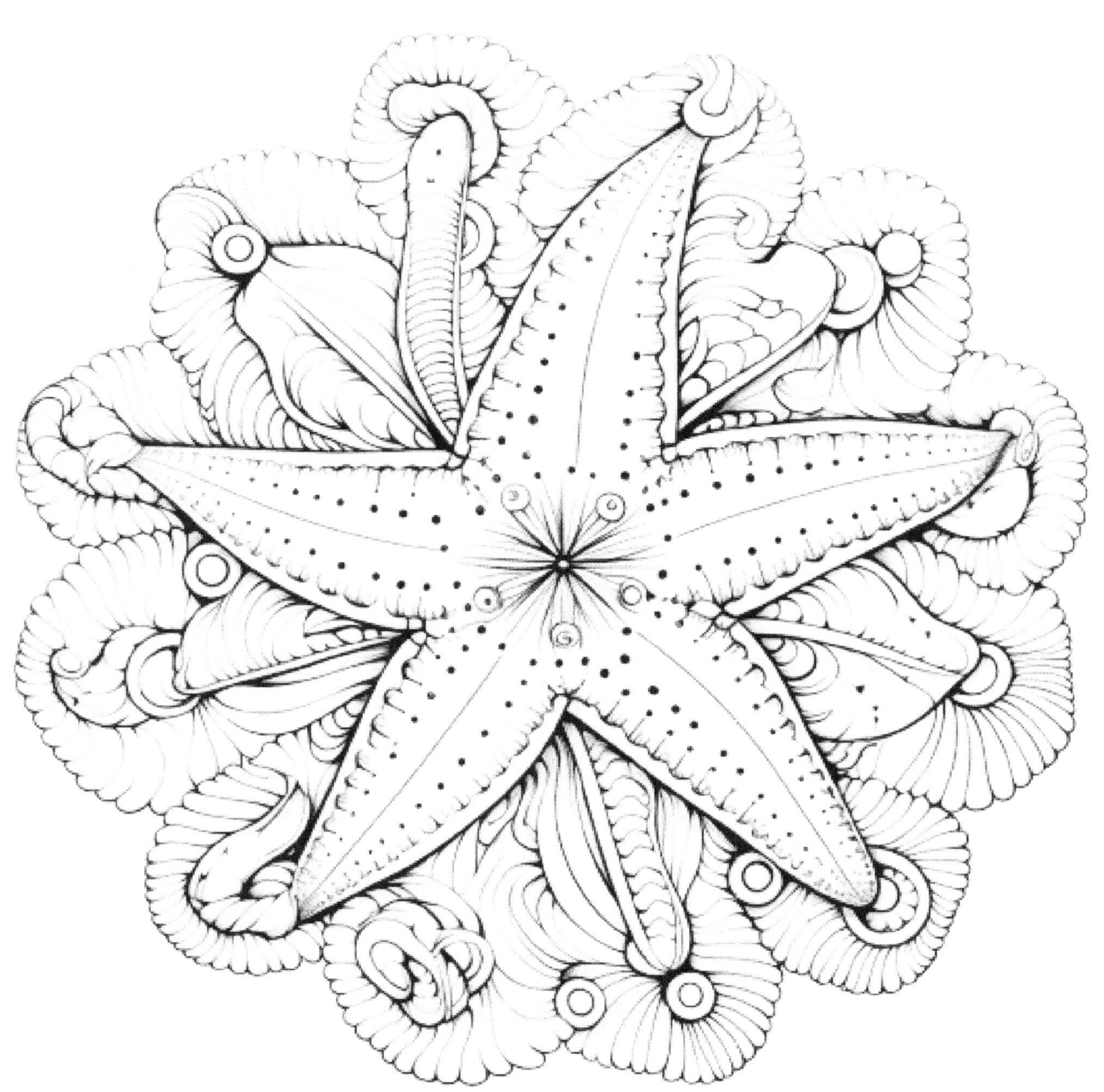

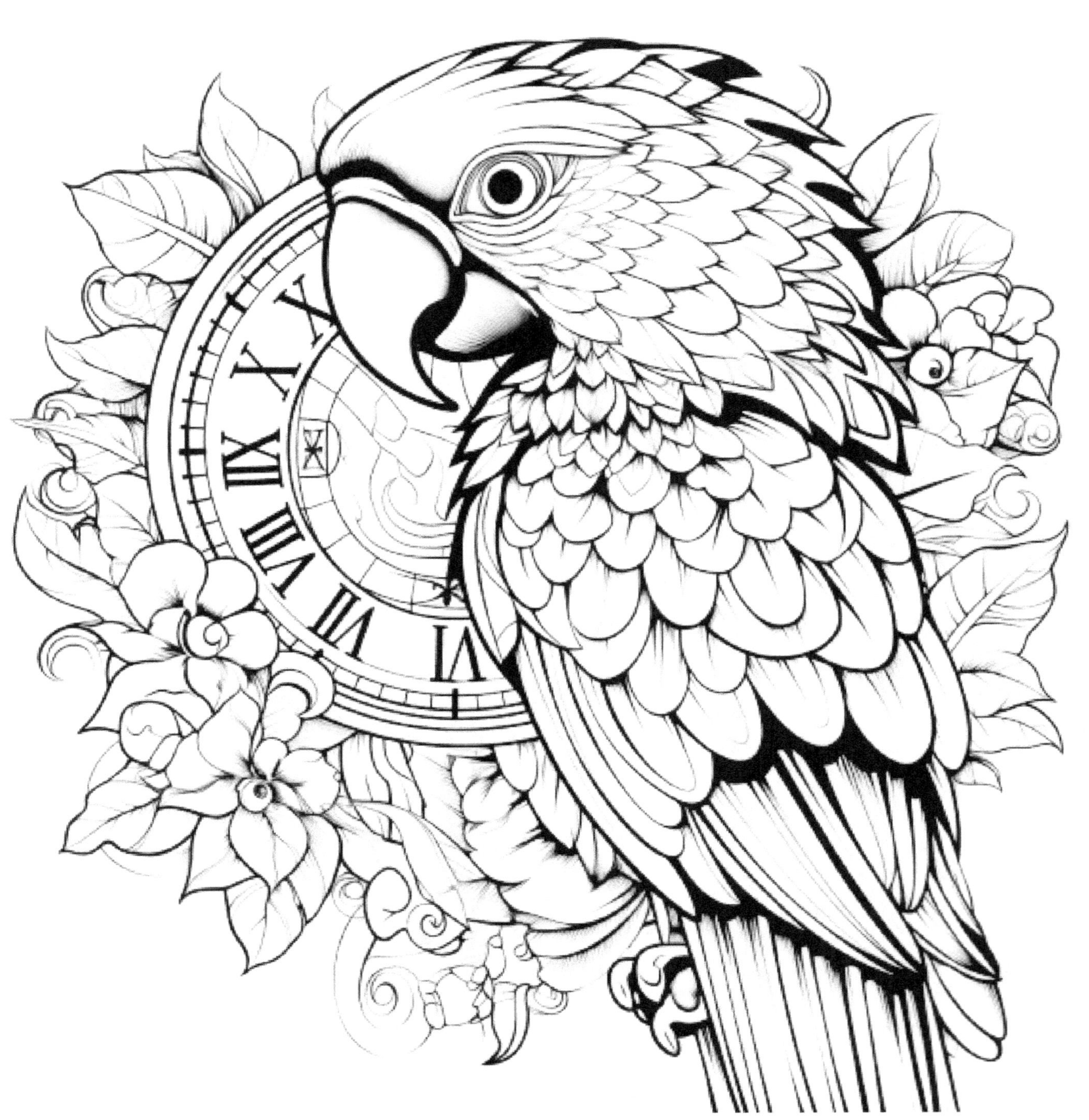

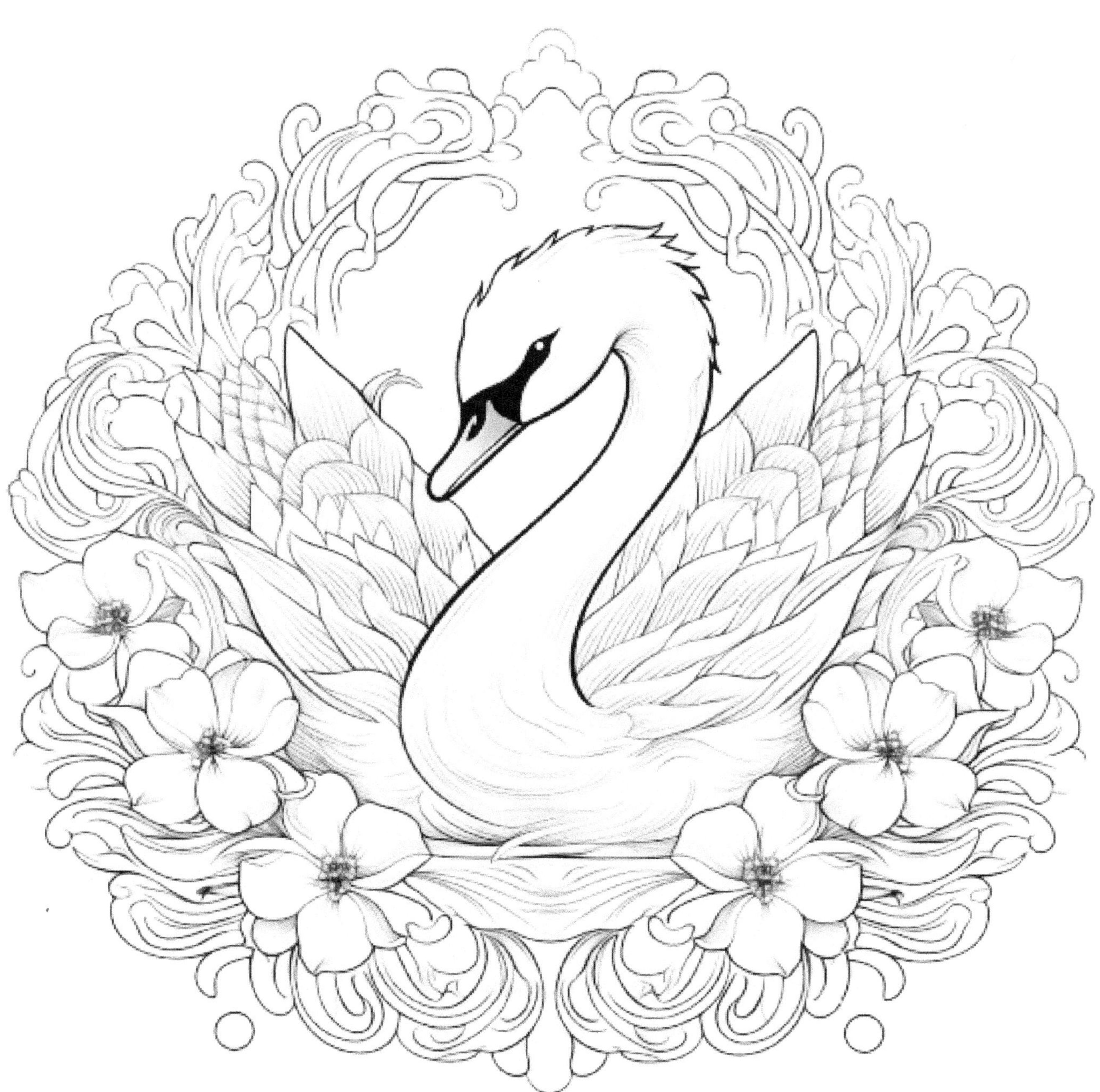

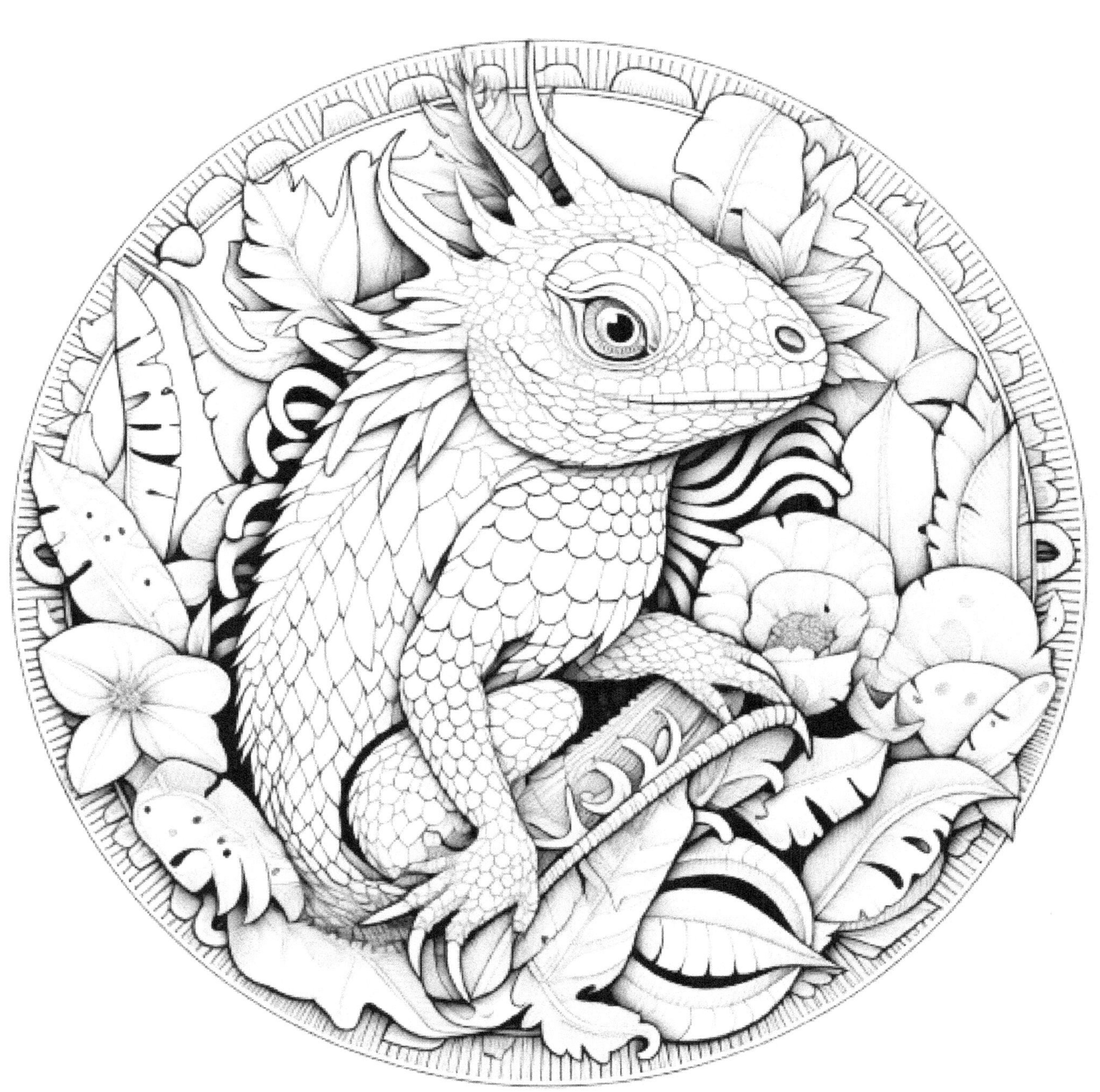

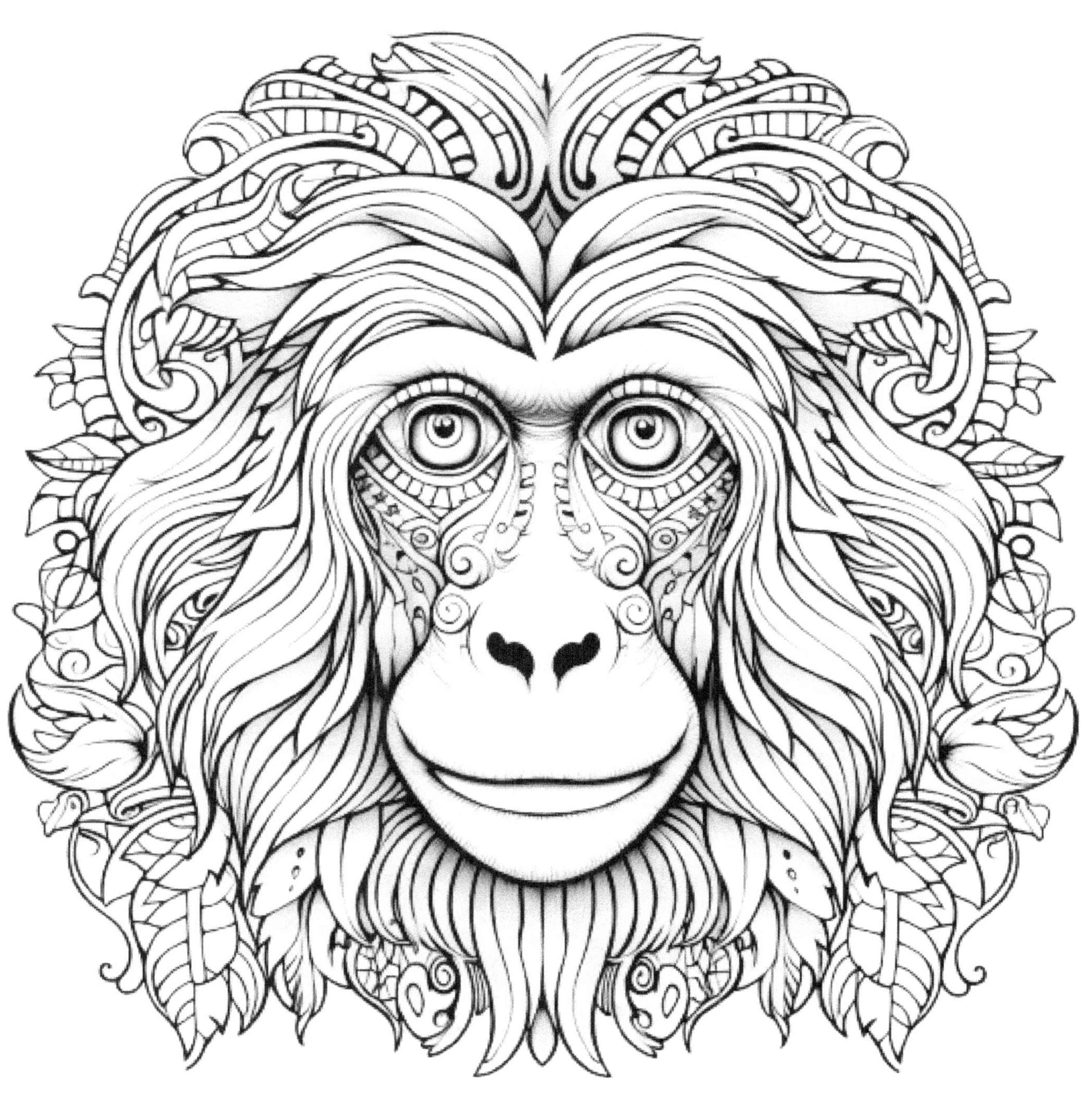

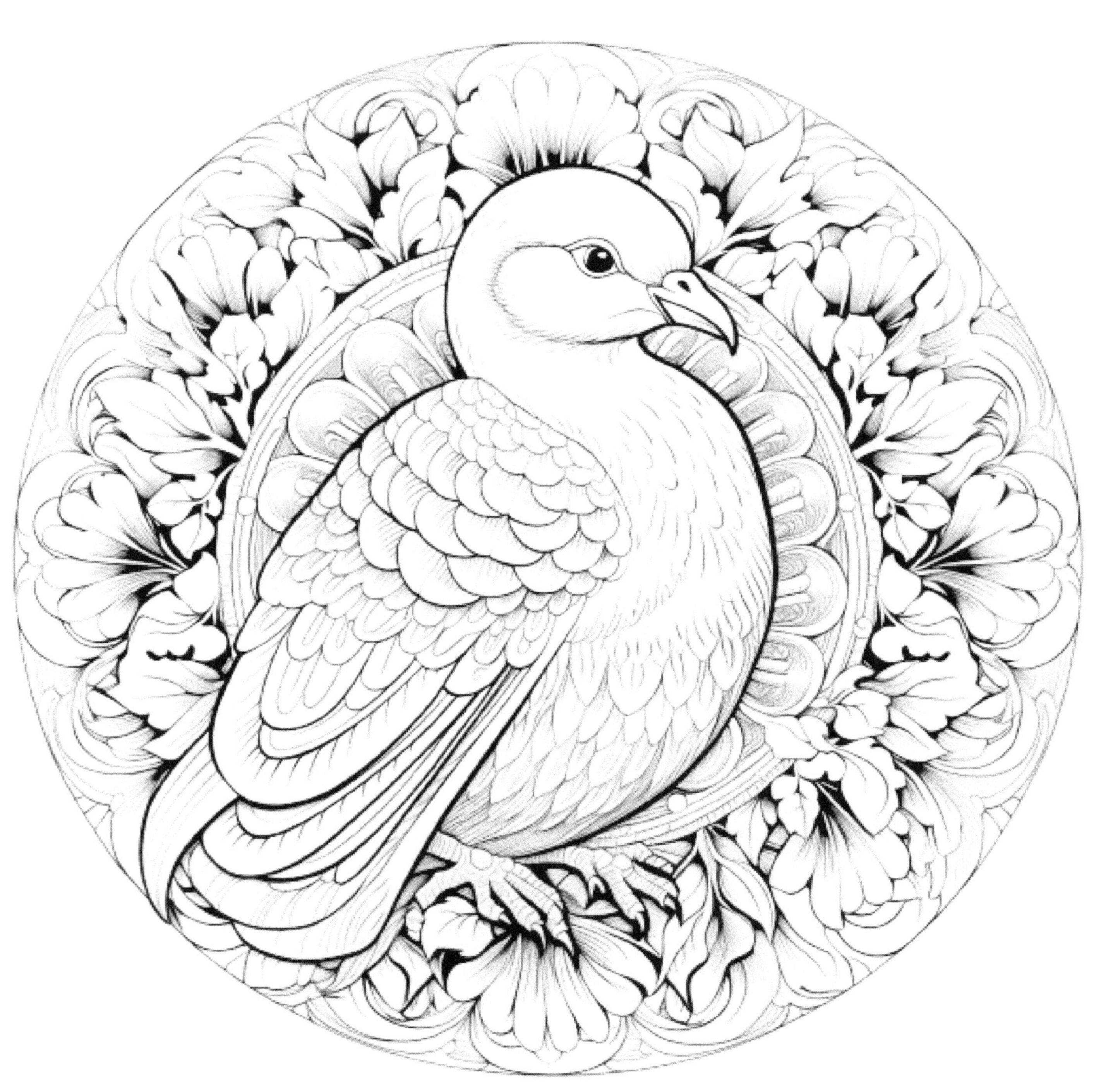

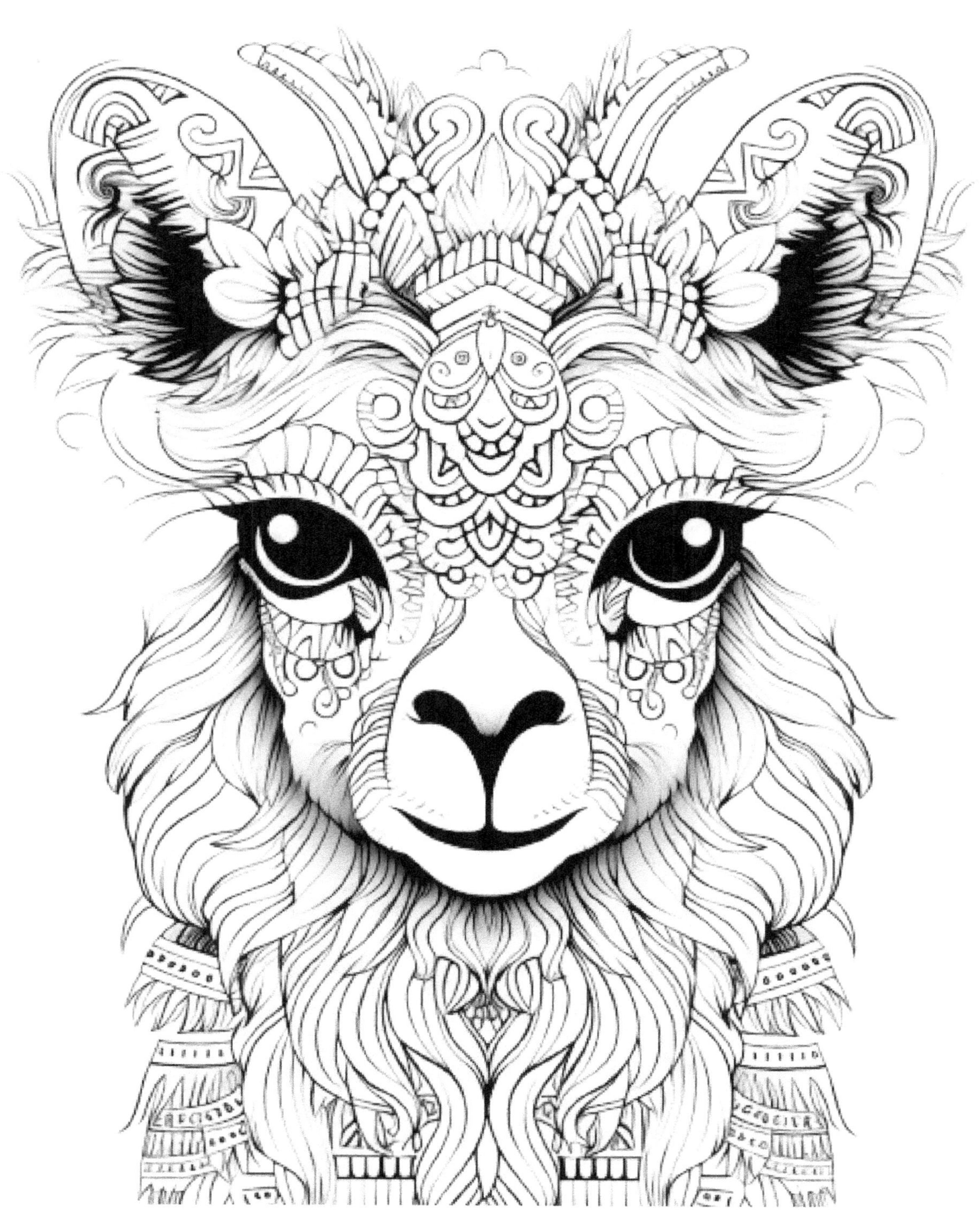

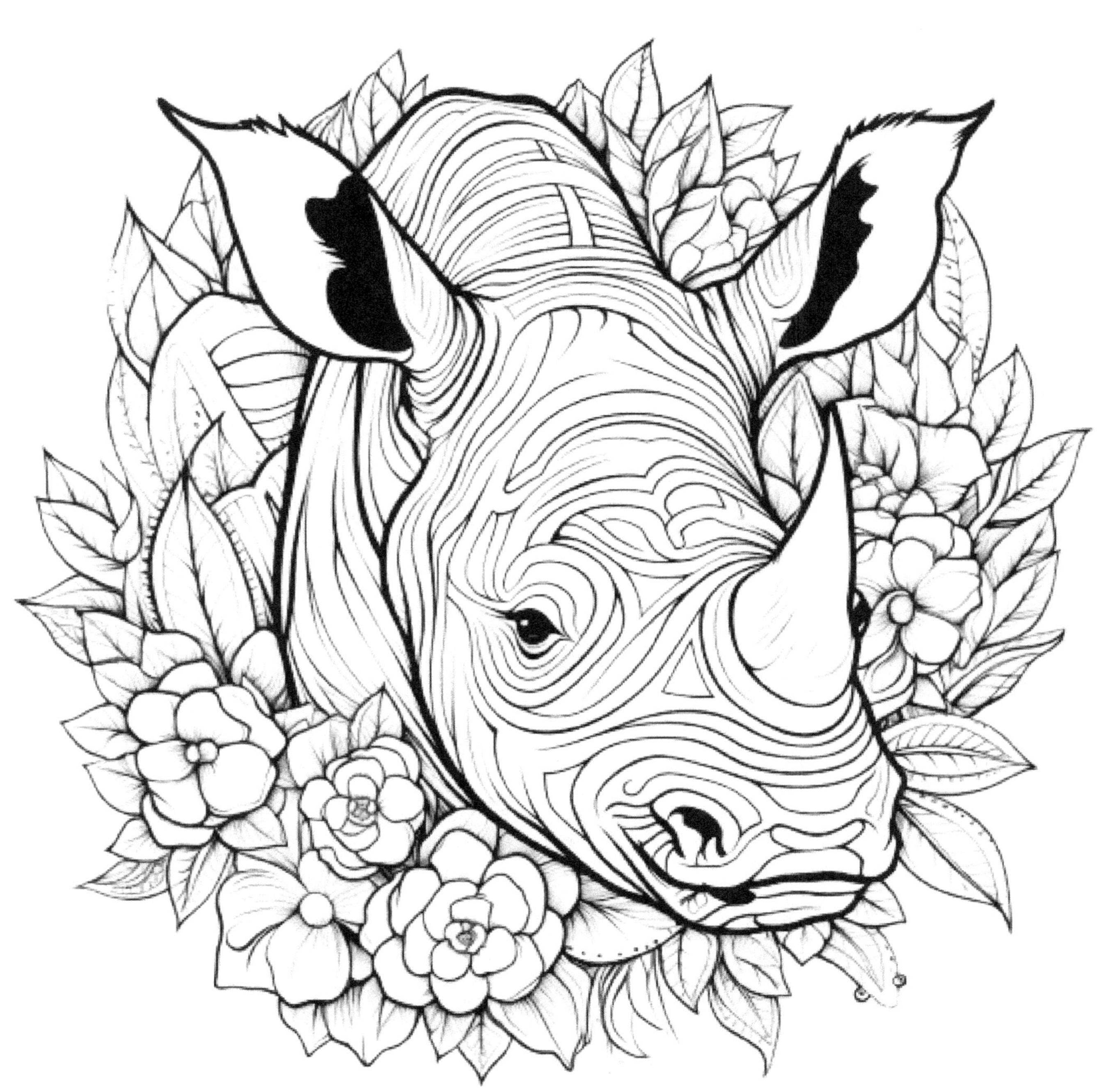

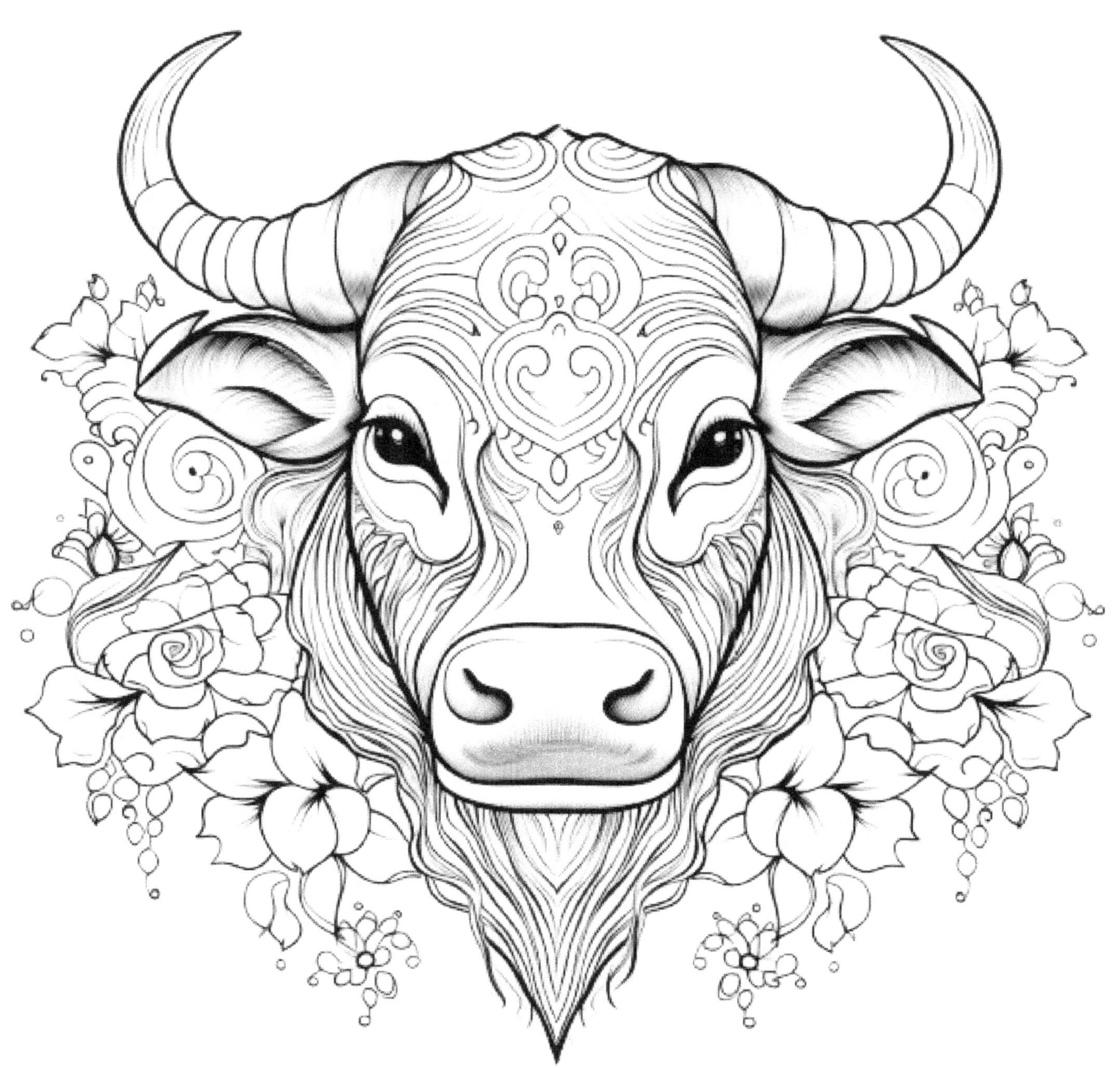

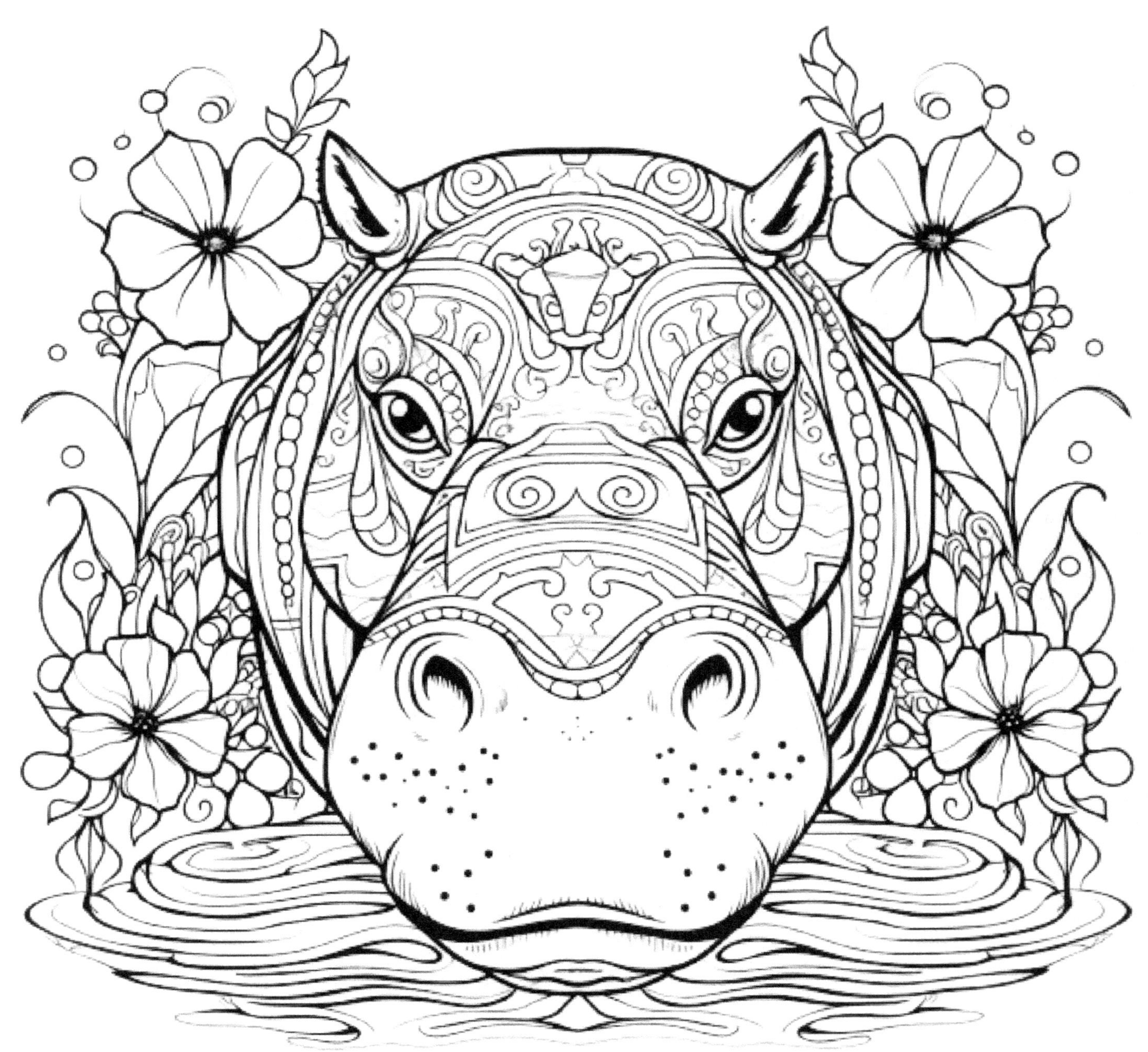

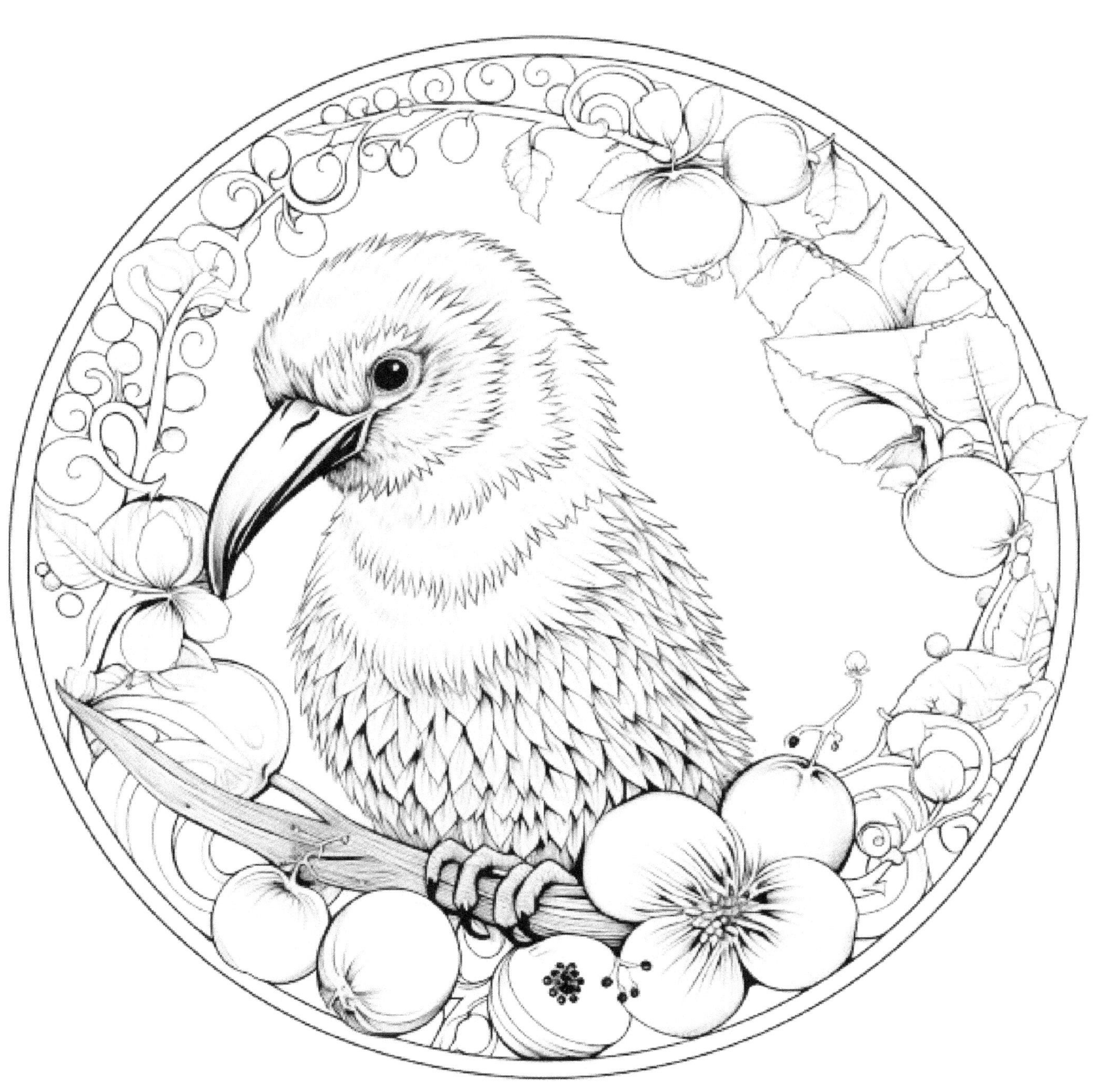

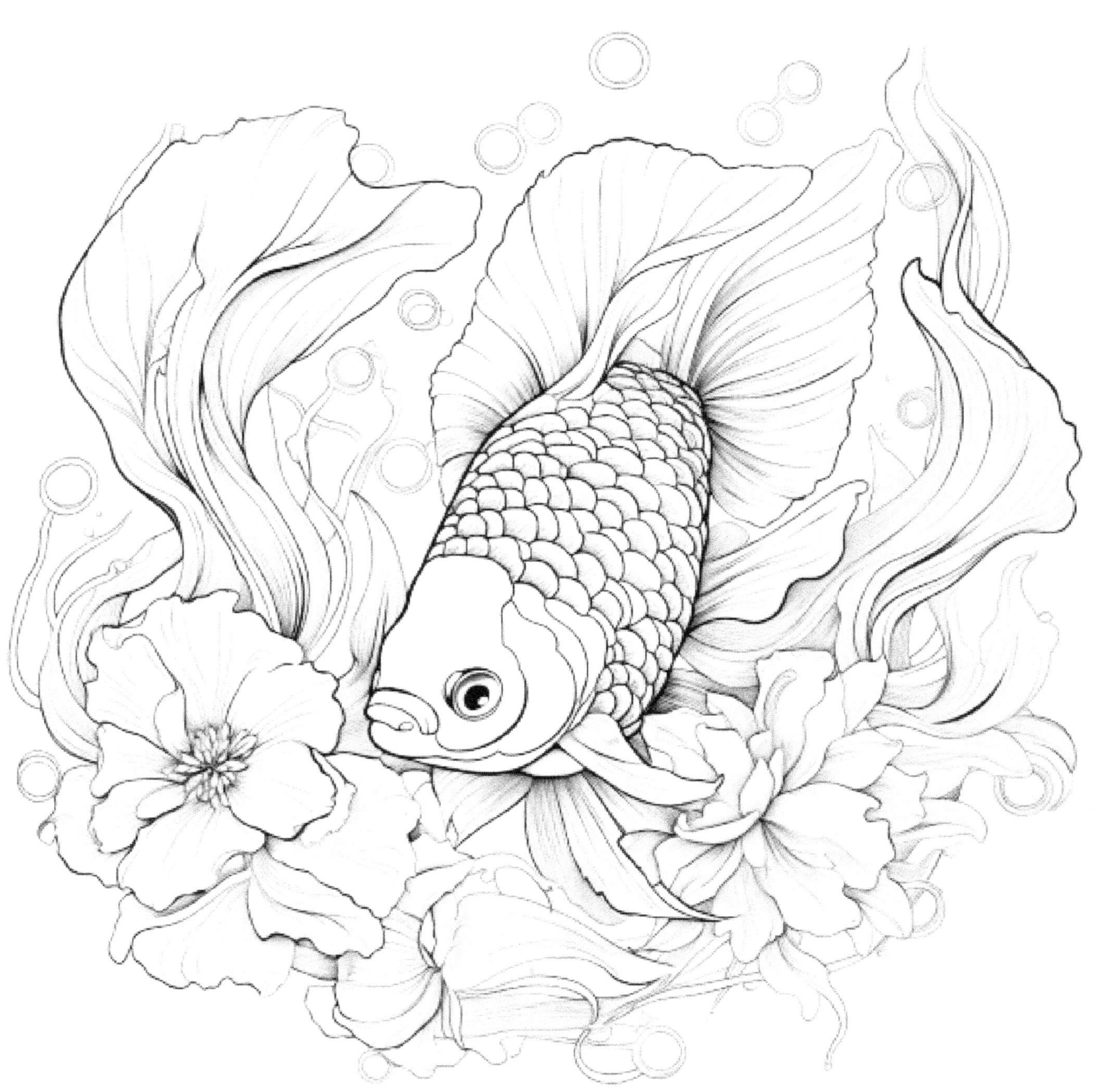

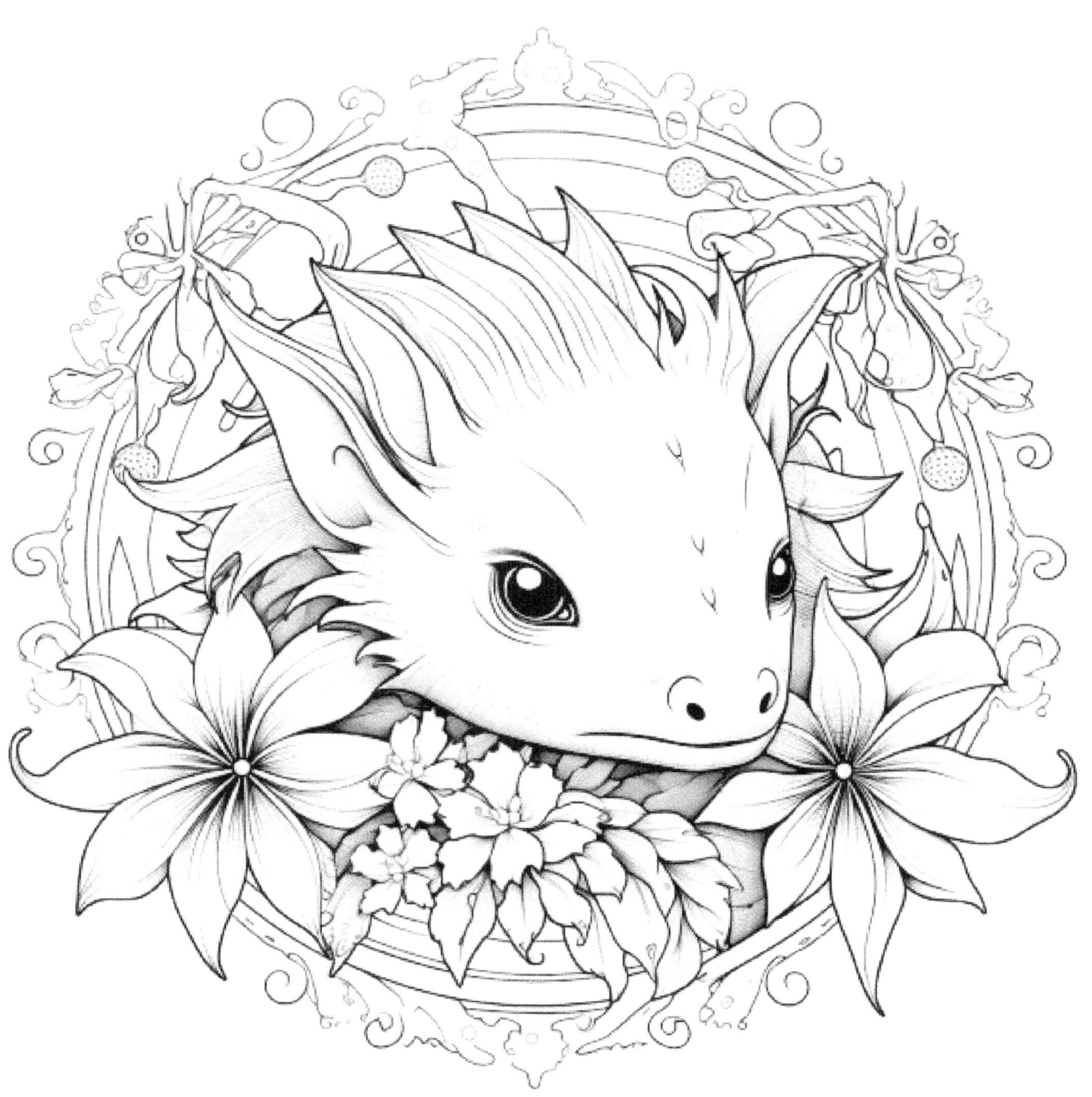

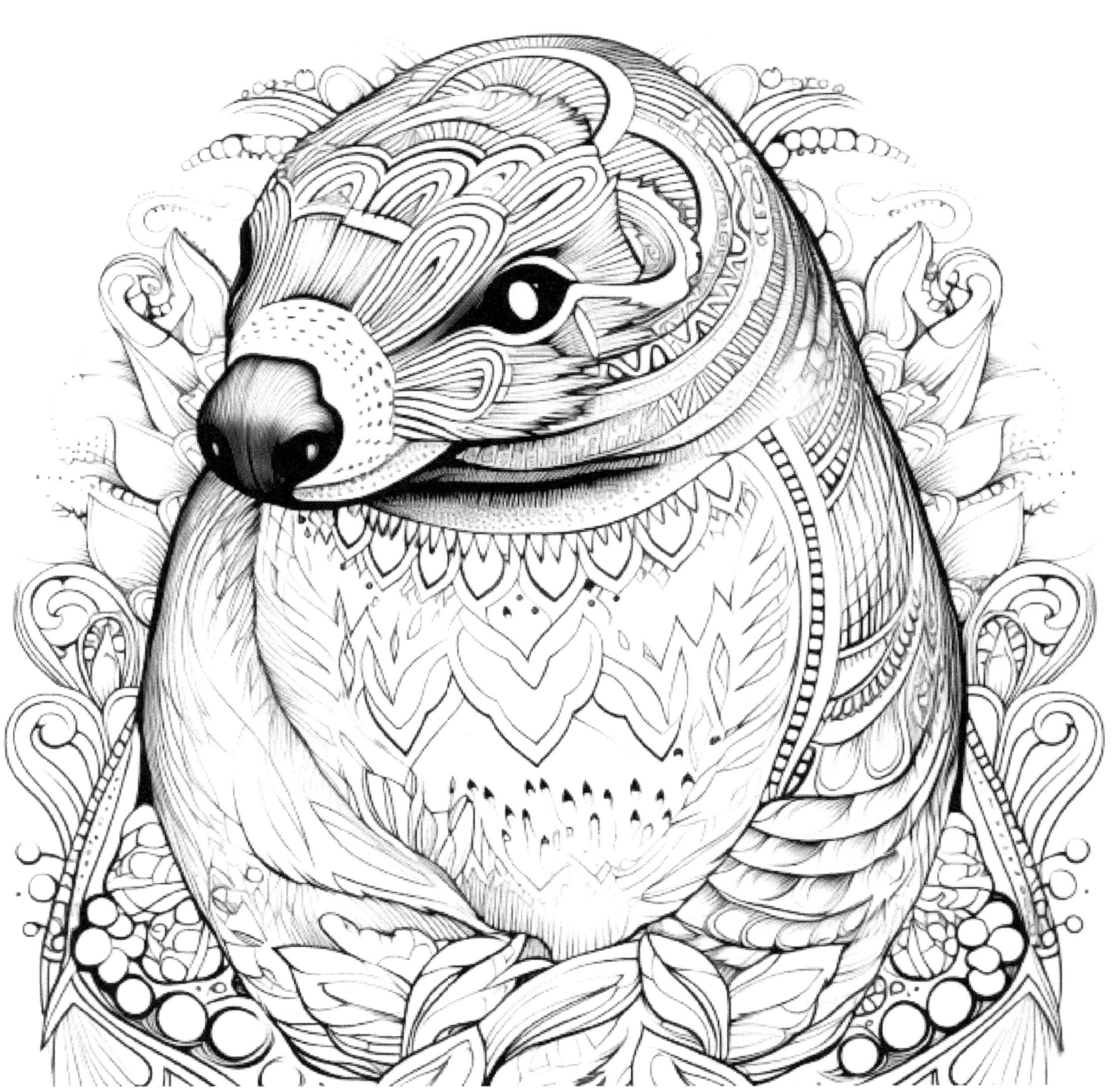

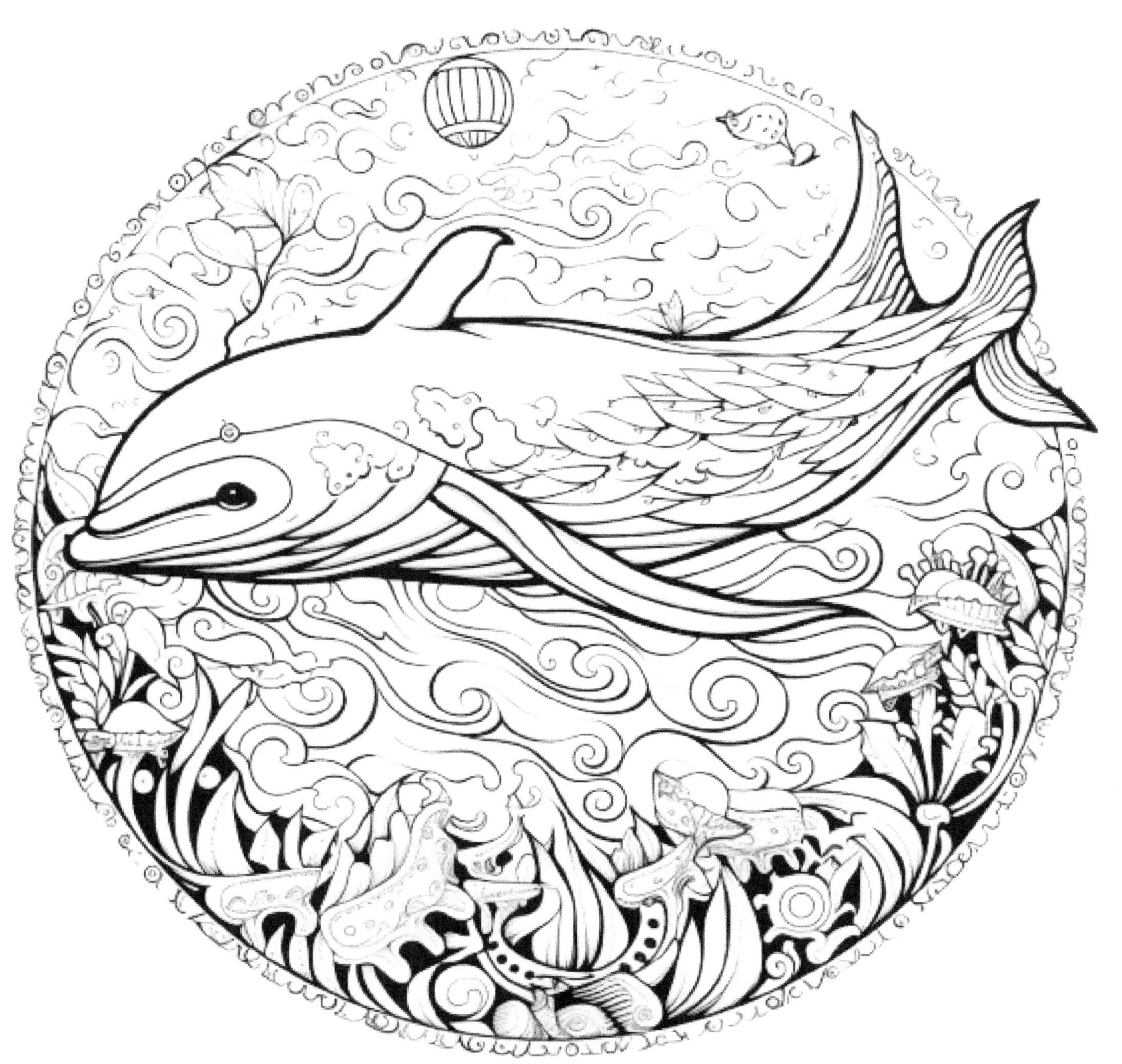

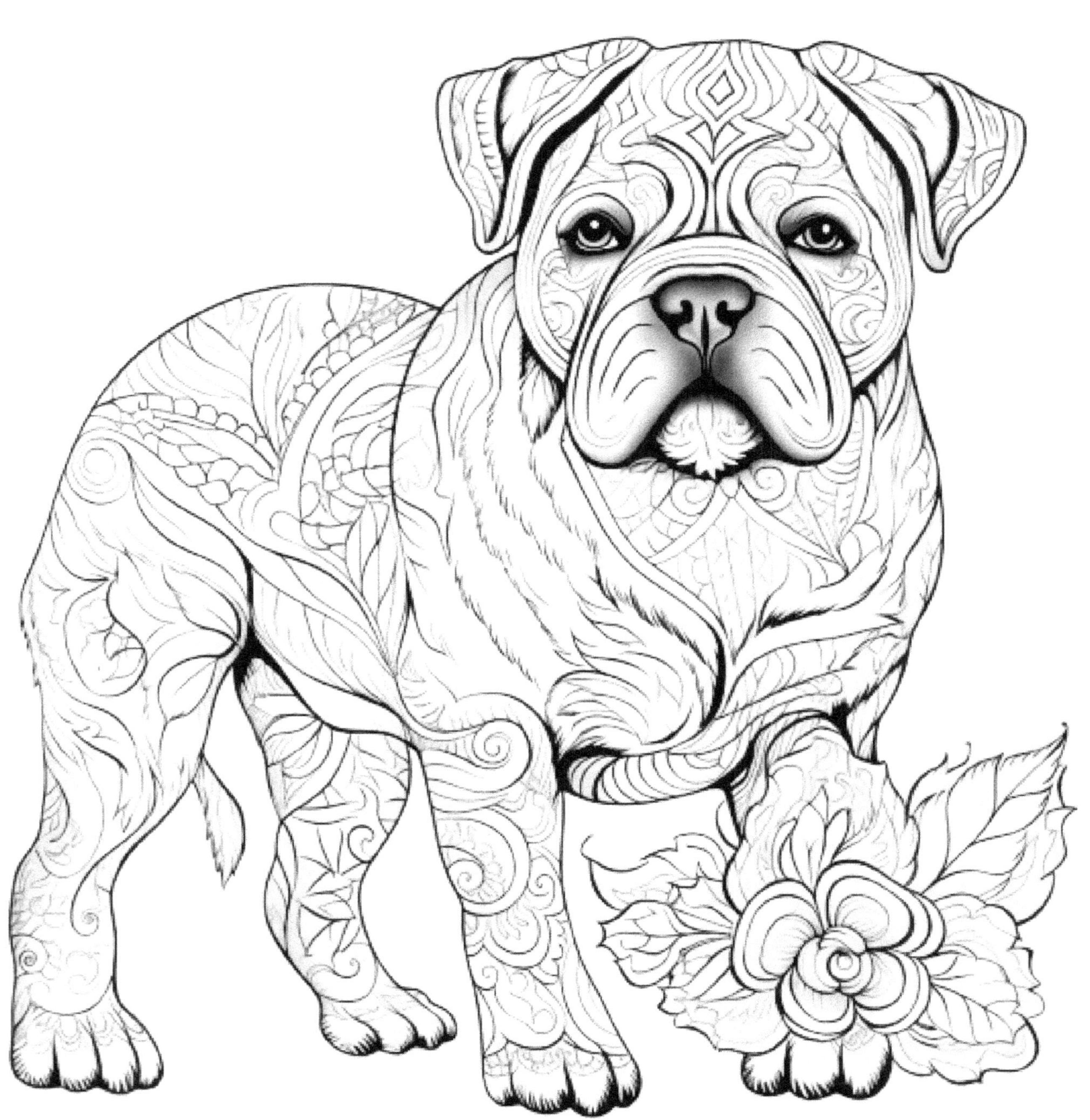

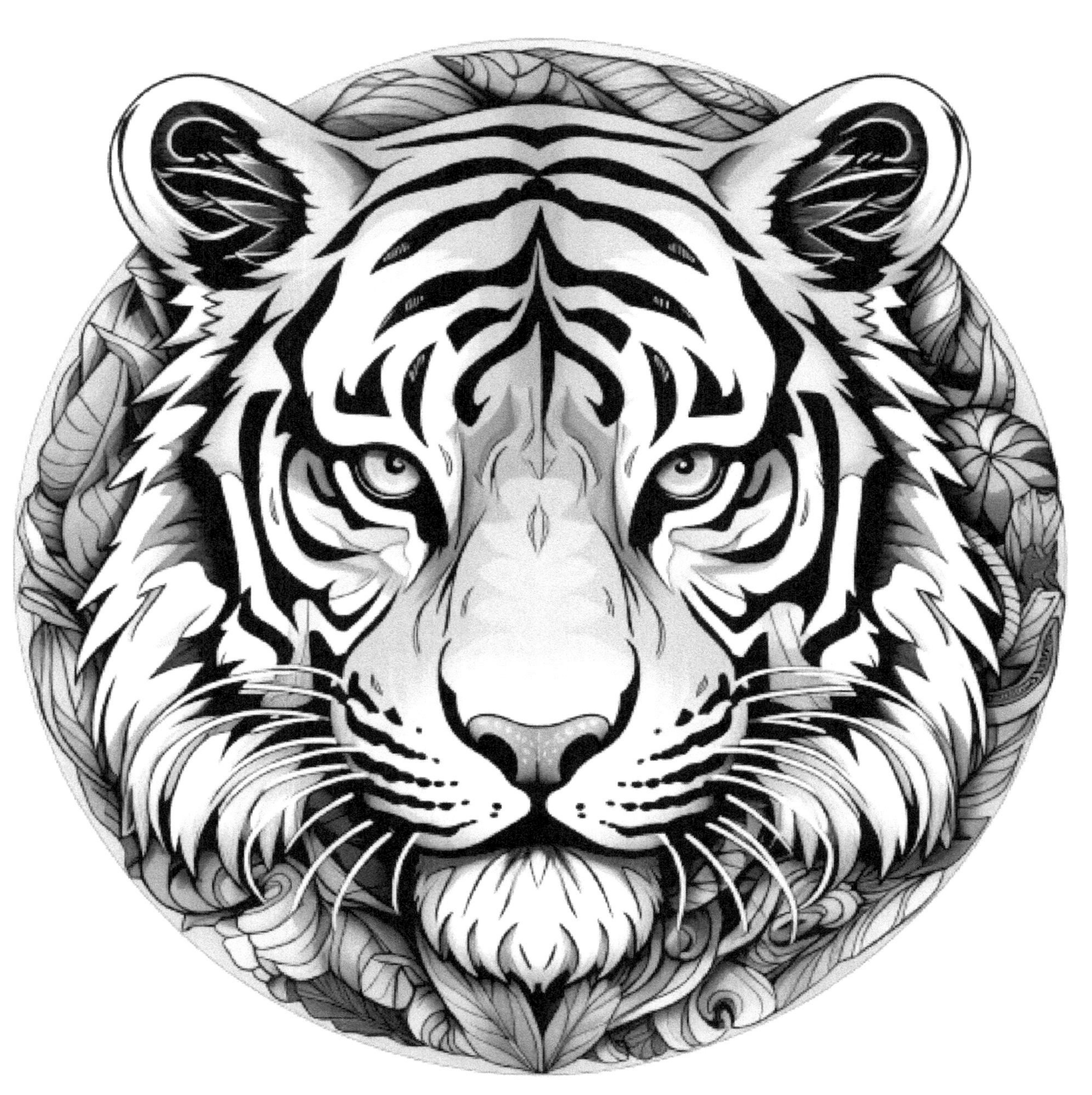

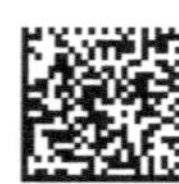